GOWESTY
7PRN880

Exploring All the National Parks

ROAMING AMERICA

Renee & Matthew Hahnel

Lannoo

Capitol Reef

ROAMING AMERICA

Our journey to all the national parks

Thank you for picking up our book; we are incredibly happy to be able to share this journey with you. Roaming America is the story of our visit to all the US national parks in one epic seven-month-long road trip. Like every story, it didn't just miraculously come to fruition overnight, so let's jump back to the beginning ...

We are Renee and Matthew Hahnel, travel and adventure photographers based in Seattle. We were both born and raised in Melbourne, Australia, and fate would have us meet in high school many moons ago. During the early years of our relationship, we quickly found a common interest in travel and exploring the outdoors, but little did we know what that would eventuate into.

In 2012 we embarked on our first trip to the USA, and it was our visits to places like Yosemite, Mount Rainier and Glacier that sparked a deep love for the national parks. We returned home and immediately applied for the Diversity Visa Program, which is essentially a lottery system to win permanent residency in the US.

Luck was in our favour, and in 2014 our names came up in the lottery, giving us a chance to move to America after rigorous interviews, background checks, and medical tests. So, in early 2015 we boarded a flight bound for Colorado with our lives packed into a few suitcases and almost no plans.

We immediately took to living in the mountains and cherished every weekend that allowed us to hike, take photos, and adventure to new places. Gradually our work as photographers began to replace our 9-to-5 jobs and we were eventually able to pursue our dream careers full-time. This is where the national parks road trip comes into the scene ...

It was a week before Christmas in 2016 when we received an email that immediately sparked our interest. It was from Evolve, a previous client of ours that were launching a new product. Part of the proceeds were to be donated to the National Parks Foundation in an effort to protect our natural spaces. They suggested a collaboration where they would send us to every single national park in an effort to bring awareness to their brand and mission. We honestly thought they were joking at first.

Initially, it was unclear how long this hypothetical and monumental adventure would take ... or if it was even possible. We were given a week to find out. The logistics of putting together a trip like this was not easy and we spent hours tirelessly researching all the possibilities. Finally, a week later, we got back to Evolve with a plan of how this could all come together. We proposed a trip route that would have us visit all 59 US national parks in only seven months. It was only when they said yes that it actually hit home ... that we would be taking this once-in-a-lifetime trip together.

On 1 April 2017 we arrived at Go Westy in California to pick up our van Ruby, a 1988 Westfalia Vanagon that would become our home for a good part of that year. We set off for our first national park, Grand Canyon, with a document listing our route, a few campsites booked here and there, and big expectations for how it would all pan out. Needless to say, we were in for one heck of a ride, and the months that followed shaped us immensely as individuals, a couple, and creatives.

Our journey saw us travel 25,000+ miles/40,000+ km, across 39 states, to two US territories, on 26 flights, and along countless hiking trails. Despite all the incredible experiences we were able to have, this was ultimately a working trip for us, and those seven months turned out to be the most rewarding and exhausting days of our lives.

We surprisingly didn't have too many hiccups along the way, with only a few van breakdowns and a couple of delayed flights slightly setting us back. We did, however, have our fair share of uncomfortable moments … like the time we woke to mice running up our blankets in the van, the heart-stopping grizzly bear encounters in Alaska, and that time we caught a tropical illness in the Virgin Islands.

As you would imagine, the special moments we experienced far outweighed the bad. We had to pinch ourselves during nights where we would fall asleep under a blanket of stars, or those times we stood on mountain summits watching a golden sunset, and every day that we had the privilege of waking up somewhere new and exciting.

Living in the van taught us to get by with less. We recycled through the same outfits day in, day out, slept cramped up next to each other every night, cooked basic meals, and went without comforts like TV and a proper desk to work at. Instead, we replaced these things with new experiences, the chance to journal and reflect, to meet interesting people, and to spend quality time together as a couple.

This book is the result of not only our seven-month journey to all the national parks, but the countless hours of editing photographs, recording our memories, and working out how to best share our story. We hope you feel a connection to the national parks as you read through these pages, and ultimately, we hope this book inspires you to take more adventures and be a steward for protecting this beautiful world we call home.

Renee + Matthew

@ReneeRoaming *@MatthewHahnel*
reneeroaming.com *matthewhahnel.com*

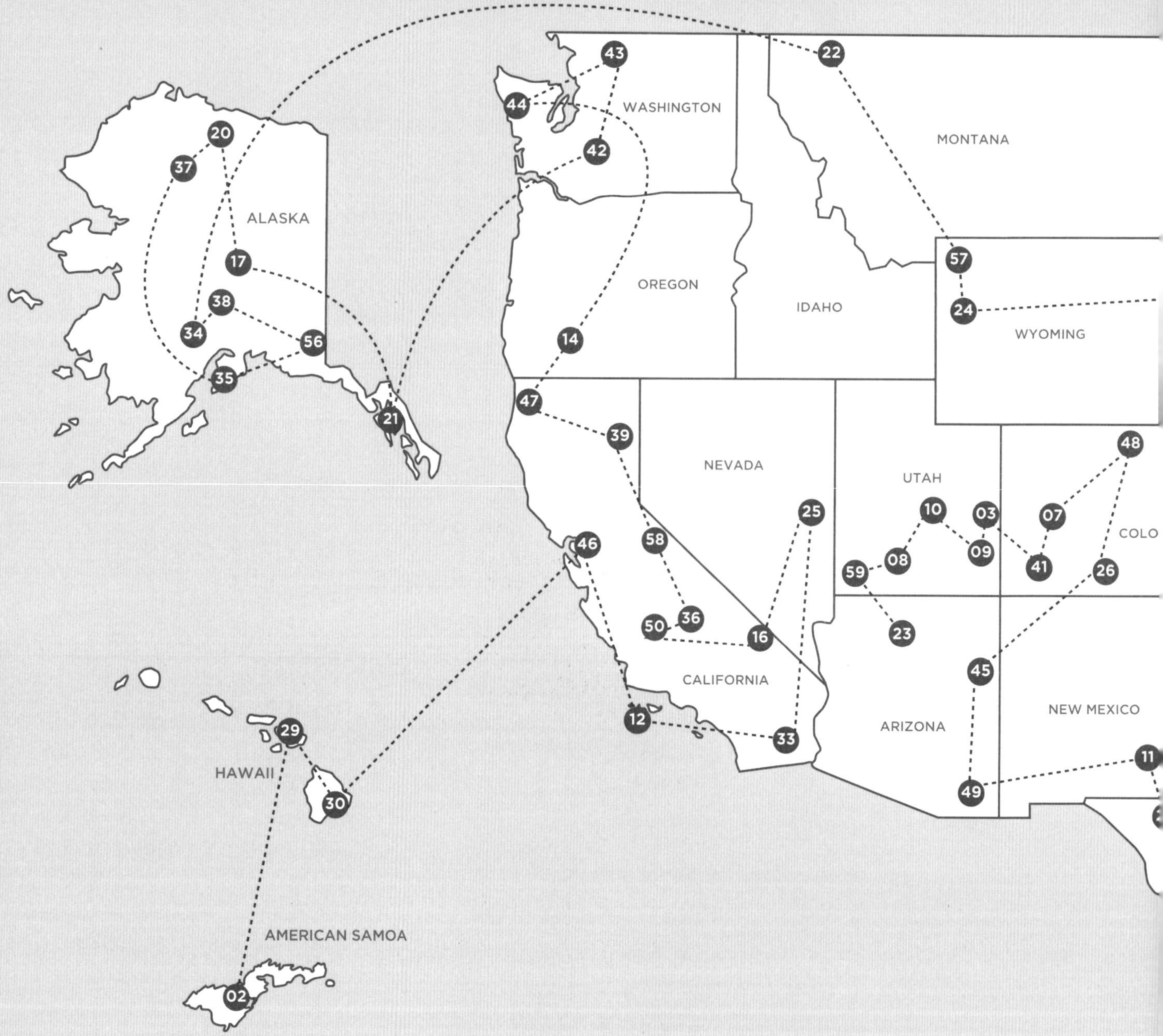

OUR 7-MONTH TRIP ITINERARY

Route To See All The National Parks

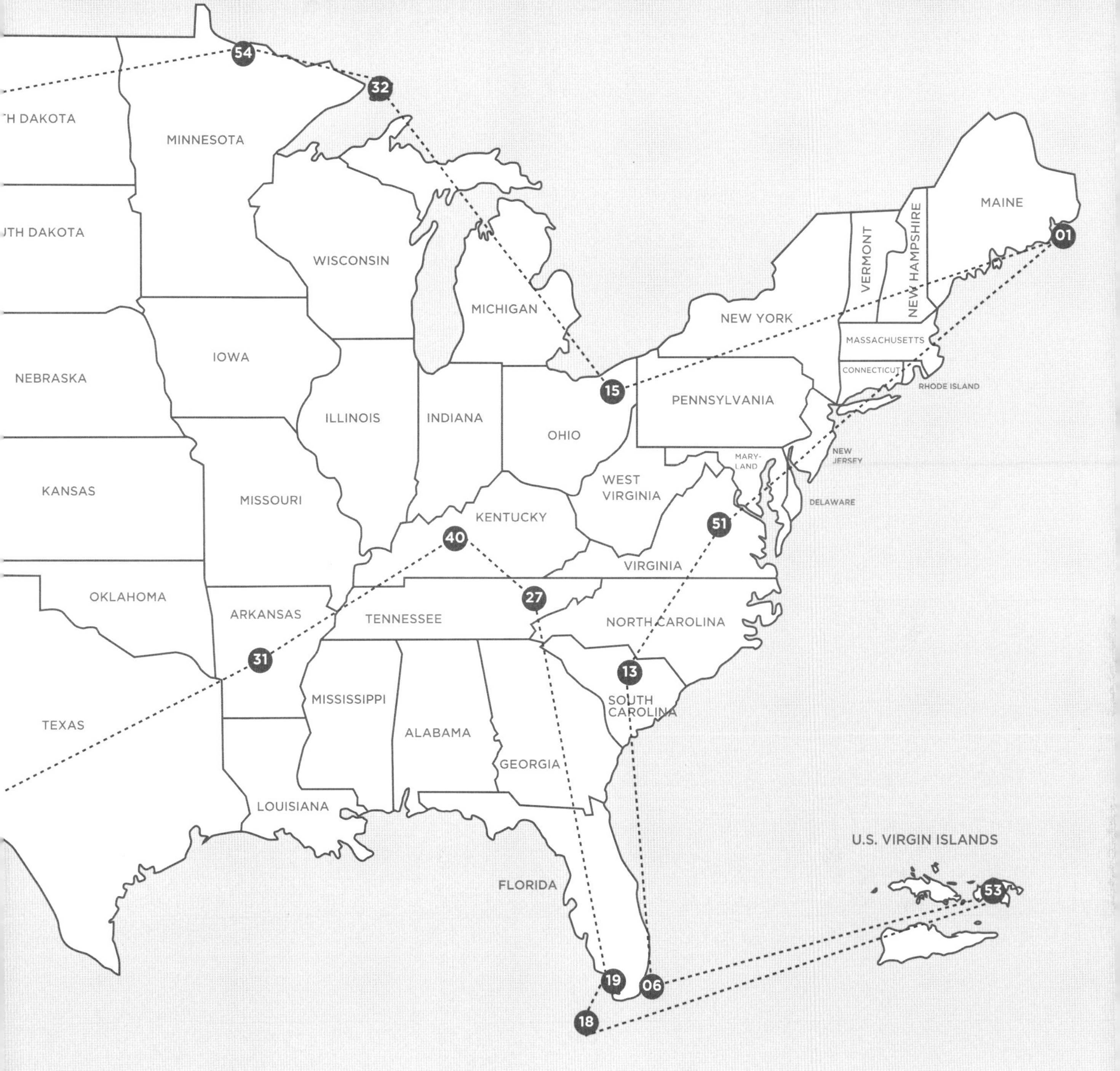

01 Acadia
02 American Samoa
03 Arches
04 Badlands
05 Big Bend
06 Biscayne
07 Black Canyon of the Gunnison
08 Bryce Canyon
09 Canyonlands
10 Capitol Reef
11 Carlsbad Caverns
12 Channel Islands
13 Congaree
14 Crater Lake
15 Cuyahoga Valley
16 Death Valley
17 Denali
18 Dry Tortugas
19 Everglades
20 Gates of the Arctic
21 Glacier Bay
22 Glacier
23 Grand Canyon
24 Grand Teton
25 Great Basin
26 Great Sand Dunes
27 Great Smoky Mountains
28 Guadalupe Mountains
29 Haleakalā
30 Hawai'i Volcanoes
31 Hot Springs
32 Isle Royal
33 Joshua Tree
34 Katmai
35 Kenai Fjords
36 Kings Canyon
37 Kobuk Valley
38 Lake Clark
39 Lassen Volcanic
40 Mammoth Cave
41 Mesa Verde
42 Mount Rainier
43 North Cascades
44 Olympic
45 Petrified Forest
46 Pinnacles
47 Redwood
48 Rocky Mountain
49 Saguaro
50 Sequoia
51 Shenandoah
52 Theodore Roosevelt
53 Virgin Islands
54 Voyageurs
55 Wind Cave
56 Wrangell-St. Elias
57 Yellowstone
58 Yosemite
59 Zion

he numbers on the map correspond with the chapter numbers.

NATIONAL PARKS

Extras

“I felt my lungs inflate with the onrush of scenery, air, mountains, trees, people. I thought, ‘This is what it is to be happy.’”

– *Sylvia Plath*

Badlands

Rocky Mountain

01

ACADIA NATIONAL PARK

New England's Finest

Visitors flock to Acadia National Park to experience a vibrant coastline, unique wildlife, and the highest point along the North Atlantic Seaboard: Cadillac Mountain. The quaint town of Bar Harbor is located just minutes from Acadia, and many visitors come to the area to sample the fresh local seafood, stroll around the downtown precinct, and explore the park. Acadia is popular in the summer for scenic driving, bicycling, kayaking, camping, boating, and swimming, whereas winter draws crowds for cross-country skiing and snowshoeing.

LOCATION Maine
PARK SIZE 49,052 acres
ICONIC FEATURE Cadillac Mountain
BEST SEASON Summer and fall

VISIT TIME Highlights in 1-2 days, or best explored in 3-4 days
STAY Camp at the Blackwoods Campground, or stay in nearby Bar Harbor.
MUST HIKE Bass Harbor Head Lighthouse and the North Bubble trails
PHOTO TIP Capture sunrise at Jordan Pond and Cadillac Mountain, and sunset at the Bass Harbor Head Lighthouse.

"All sleepiness is briefly forgotten as we stand at the summit of Cadillac Mountain and watch the sun slowly glow over the Atlantic."

Exhaustion doesn't begin to describe just how tired we are. It's the kind of sleep deprivation that leaves you unbalanced physically and mentally, struggling to make even the most basic decisions. It's 4 a.m. and our alarm goes off inside the van... Sunrises are early in Acadia during mid-June. We haul ourselves out of bed and out into the crisp Maine air. All sleepiness is briefly forgotten as we stand at the summit of Cadillac Mountain and watch the sun slowly glow over the Atlantic. Just us and maybe 15 others are the first people in the entire country to witness sunrise that day.

02

NATIONAL PARK OF AMERICAN SAMOA

South Pacific Tropical Paradise

The National Park of American Samoa is quietly tucked away in the Pacific Ocean, some 2,600 mi / 4,200 km southwest of Hawai'i. The park is bursting with beautiful beaches, rare plants and animals, extraordinary coral reefs, and a rich culture. Spread out across three islands – Tutuila, Ta'ū, and Ofu – transport between different areas and tourist infrastructure are still being developed, though the locals are friendly and welcoming to visitors. These islands are vibrant in every sense of the word, from the lively people, lush hiking trails, deep blue waters, and magnificently colorful sunsets. They may just be America's best-kept secret.

LOCATION U.S. Territory of American Samoa
PARK SIZE 13,500 acres
ICONIC FEATURE Views of Tutuila from the Mount Alava Trail
BEST SEASON Year round
VISIT TIME Best explored in 3-5 days

STAY The National Park Service runs a homestay program, allowing visitors to have a first-hand experience of the Samoan culture.
MUST HIKE Pola Island Trail and Mount Alava Trail
PHOTO TIP The island of Ofu provides incredible photo opportunities above and below the water. On the island of Tutuila, picturesque locations include Vatia Bay, Afono Pass, Afono Bay, and Mount Alava.

"These islands are vibrant in every sense of the word, from the lively people, lush foliage, deep blue waters, and magnificently colorful sunsets. They may just be America's best-kept secret."

Our time exploring Tutuila is bittersweet, for it's the last stop on our seven-month journey to all of America's national parks. We spend our days hiking rainforest trails, sampling local food, cooling off in the Pacific Ocean, and learning about Samoan culture. Our fondest memory is watching sunset on the beach during our last night on Tutuila. The sky was so deeply orange and red that it almost appeared as if it were on fire. Local children played around us on the beach, laughing and splashing in pure joy. What a privilege it was to witness such a scene.

03

ARCHES NATIONAL PARK

Rock Formations For Days

Conveniently located just north of Moab, Arches National Park is home to some of the most impressive rock formations in the country, and some 2,000 natural sandstone arches. This relatively small park can easily be toured by car in a single day, though spending a little longer exploring the trails and experiencing the arches up close is recommended. Nearby Canyonlands National Park, the La Sal mountains, and the Colorado River are popular attractions to pair with a trip to Arches. This corner of the Southwest is a stomping ground for those who love hiking, camping, climbing, canyoning, dirt-biking, whitewater rafting, and photography.

LOCATION Utah
PARK SIZE 76,679 acres
ICONIC FEATURE Delicate Arch
BEST SEASON Fall through early spring
VISIT TIME Highlights in 1-2 days, or best explored in 2-3 days

STAY Camp at the Devils Garden, or stay in nearby Moab.
MUST HIKE Windows Loop and Turret Arch Trail
PHOTO TIP Capture Delicate Arch at sunset, and stay out until the stars come out. This is one of the best spots in the world for astrophotography.

Beeeep beeeeeeep. It's 2 a.m. and our alarm is screaming at us to wake up after only a few hours of rest. Hauling ourselves out of the van, we set off to witness and photograph the Milky Way above Delicate Arch. Our headlamps guide the way as we battle sleepiness and navigate over rocks and ledges. We soon arrive at the arch, set down our heavy camera bags, and turn off our headlamps. I will never forget the sight and feeling of what we witness in the moments after. It's as if we are gazing up at every star that has ever existed and will ever exist, like there is barely a gap between to allow for darkness. The Milky Way is rising directly above the arch and it's one of the most beautiful spectacles any of us have experienced.

"I will never forget the sight and feeling of what we witness in the moments after. It's as if we are gazing up at every star that has ever existed and will ever exist, like there is barely a gap between to allow for darkness."

04

BADLANDS NATIONAL PARK

Wild, Unearthly, & Unfathomable

Badlands National Park is one of those wild, unearthly, and almost unfathomable places that we presume only exist in fiction. Visitors are lured to the park by striking rock formations, the chance to explore ancient natural history, and countless photographic opportunities. Diversity is the theme of the park, with fossils, prairie, wildlife, Lakota history, pioneer history, and homesteading life all waiting to be explored. Badlands National Park is open year-round, though the months of June–August can see very warm temperatures and busy crowds. Visiting in the shoulder seasons will be your best bet for comfortable weather and more solitude.

LOCATION South Dakota
PARK SIZE 244,000 acres
ICONIC FEATURE Badlands Loop State Scenic Byway
BEST SEASON Spring and fall
VISIT TIME Best explored in 1-2 days
STAY Cedar Pass Lodge or Cedar Pass Campground
MUST HIKE The Notch Trail
PHOTO TIP Capture sunrise and sunset at Big Badlands Overlook, and astrophotography from White River Valley Overlook.

"The Badlands grade all the way from those that are almost rolling in character to those that are so fantastically broken in form and so bizarre in color as to seem hardly properly to belong to this earth."

– *Theodore Roosevelt*

We have been told that Badlands can experience unpredictable weather, but we are not expecting what happens our last afternoon exploring the park. It all starts with a quiet stroll along the Notch Trail. The sun is shining and there isn't a breath of wind. The weather begins to change as we head back to the campsite for an early dinner. Before we know it, we are in the middle of a full-blown storm. Tents are becoming unhinged and flying across the campground, the skies darken around us, and rain begins to pour down. The storm passes as quickly as it arrived, suddenly greeting us with a mesmerizing rainbow over the badlands. We spend the night watching storms roll by in the distance and what feels like endless lightning bolts scattering the prairies.

05

BIG BEND NATIONAL PARK

Hidden Gem Of The South

Big Bend was one of the most beautiful and surprising parks of our entire trip. Most Americans haven't even heard of Big Bend and it's rarely listed as one of the top parks to visit, making its secluded beauty even more special. The famous Rio Grande River runs through the park and provides a natural boundary between the United States and Mexico. The two nations meet in a setting of wild mountains and desert, sharing some of the most expansive and diverse vistas in the world. Big Bend is also one of the largest parks in the country and varies in elevation, ranging from 1,800 ft / 550 m above sea level along the Rio Grande to nearly 8,000 ft / 2,400 m up in the Chisos Mountains.

LOCATION Texas
PARK SIZE 801,163 acres
ICONIC FEATURE Rio Grande River
BEST SEASON Fall through spring
VISIT TIME Highlights in 1-2 days, or best explored in 3-4 days

STAY Camp at Rio Grande Village, or Chisos Basin Campground for close proximity to the park's highlights.
MUST HIKE Lost Mine and Boquillas Hot Springs trails
PHOTO TIP Capture golden light streaming through Santa Elena Canyon in the hours before sunset.

In the glow of dawn, we quietly make our way to the Boquillas Hot Springs for a sunrise soak. There isn't another soul around, once again emphasizing the secluded beauty of Big Bend. The sun peeks over the horizon as we dip ourselves into the 105° F / 40° C freshwater spring. Our tired muscles welcome the warmth and our busy minds instantly slow down. For hours, we lie there soaking in the beauty of the Rio Grande and the surrounding lush vegetation. As we hike out, we are lucky enough to witness wild horses drinking from the river, again in complete solitude. We marvel that more people haven't heard about this incredible park and speak of our plans to return someday soon.

"The topography of Big Bend is so barren and jagged that America's astronauts in the 1960s took field trips to the park to prepare them for landing on the moon."

– John Jameson

06

BISCAYNE NATIONAL PARK

A Water Lover's Dream

Biscayne National Park provides a tropical respite away from the hustle and bustle of nearby Miami. Covering 173,000 acres of protected land, approximately 95% of the park can be found underwater and bursting with extensive coral reefs, plentiful marine life, and subtropical vegetation. Popular activities in Biscayne include boating, diving, snorkeling, angling, picnicking, kayaking, and camping. While many locals have their own vessels, visitors can take ranger-guided boat tours out to popular places such as Boca Chita Key, or even try a snorkeling adventure in Biscayne Bay.

We have no idea what to expect from Biscayne, other than knowing the weather will be stiflingly hot and humid. A ranger calls out for our tour group to board the boat, and before we know it, we are cruising through beautiful blue waters. We aren't wrong about the weather, but the cool ocean breeze is helping to take the edge off... sort of. We explore lush mangroves and hidden coves before arriving at picturesque Boca Chita Key. The group is quick to disembark and nearly everyone heads straight to the beach with their picnics and snorkel gear. Until now, we had no idea such a paradise existed right off the shores of Miami.

LOCATION Florida
PARK SIZE 181,500 acres
ICONIC FEATURE Boca Chita Key
BEST SEASON Winter and early spring
VISIT TIME Best explored in 1-2 days
STAY Nearby Miami has an abundance of lodging options.

MUST HIKE Take a guided boat tour to Boca Chita Key and explore the island's loop trail through wooded areas and along the water.

PHOTO TIP Boca Chita's lighthouse is photogenic from the ground and also from its viewing deck. Another option is to get out in the water to photograph the park's incredible marine life and coral reef.

07

BLACK CANYON OF THE GUNNISON NATIONAL PARK

Deep, Dark, & Magnificent

Black Canyon of the Gunnison National Park is split into two main sections – the South Rim and the North Rim – with the Gunnison River running through the middle. The park contains the deepest and most dramatic sections of the Black Canyon, plunging so deep that the Empire State Building is said to fit inside vertically, not once, but twice. Most visitors explore the South Rim, due to its accessibility, services, and abundance of scenic overlooks to view the dramatic canyon walls and sheer drops.

We have been exploring the park for hours and the only people we have come across are two park rangers at the visitor center. Granted, it is early season, but this seems abnormally quiet. We find an overlook to watch the sunset and sit in wonder at the unfathomably deep canyon. They say it's so deep and narrow that sunlight only reaches the bottom for some 33 minutes each day... This place is wildly beautiful. We observe the sun lighting up the canyon walls, exposing each line and color in the rocks, almost like veins that keep this park alive.

LOCATION Colorado

PARK SIZE 30,750 acres

ICONIC FEATURE Painted Canyon

BEST SEASON Spring through fall

VISIT TIME Best explored in 1-2 days

STAY Camp at the South Rim Campground, or stay in nearby towns such as Montrose.

MUST HIKE Warner Point Trail, Rim Rock Nature Trail, and Cedar Point Nature Trail

PHOTO TIP Some of the best viewpoints for photographs are Gunnison Point and Dragon Point, often best captured at midday when the sun is streaming light down into the depths of the dark canyon.

OWESTY

ROAD TRIP ESSENTIALS

What To Pack For A National Parks Adventure

Road trips are one of the best ways to travel to the national parks. They allow you to explore the landscape on your time and see nearby destinations along the way. Your packing list will obviously vary depending on where you are going, the time of year, and the activities you are undertaking. Here are some suggestions based on what we found ourselves frequently reaching for during our own national parks road trip:

- Playlists filled with good tunes and interesting podcasts
- Snacks: nuts, granola bars, dried fruit, dark chocolate etc.
- Camera equipment and/or your phone
- Maps in printed form and also on your phone
- Hiking boots that are practical and suited to your destination
- Sun protection such as a hat, sunglasses, and sunscreen
- Reusable drink bottle to prevent plastic waste
- Mosquito repellent, plus a head net if going somewhere very buggy
- Jackets, including an insulation layer and a waterproof jacket
- Swimsuit and a lightweight quick-drying towel
- Cosy sweater and socks for those long car drives
- Small stove and a reusable mug to make hot drinks or meals
- Firewood and marshmallows, if you can legally have a campfire
- Reading material for those moments of down time
- National Park Pass: best value to purchase the annual version

08

BRYCE CANYON NATIONAL PARK

Hoodoo Heaven

Bryce Canyon often gets overshadowed by sister parks in the southwest, such as Zion and Grand Canyon. What many people don't realize until they visit is that Bryce Canyon is entirely different from these more popular parks and has endless wonders to explore. Most of the park is accessible from one main road, with the Rim Trail providing stunning views of Bryce Amphitheater and its fascinating rock formations, known as hoodoos. In fact, Bryce Canyon is home to the largest collection of hoodoos on earth, crafted over the course of millions of years. Going in on foot is the best way to explore these jagged spires, and the park provides many hiking trails offering various levels of difficulty and accessibility.

LOCATION Utah

PARK SIZE 35,835 acres

ICONIC FEATURE Bryce Amphitheater, best viewed from the Rim Trail and Sunset Point

BEST SEASON Spring and fall

VISIT TIME Highlights in 1 day, or best explored in 2-3 days

STAY Camp at North Campground, or stay in comfort at the historic Bryce Canyon Lodge.

MUST HIKE Queens Garden and Navajo Loop Trail, with the option to add on Peekaboo Loop Trail

PHOTO TIP Sunrise is the most photogenic time of the day in Bryce Canyon, best captured from Sunset Point, Inspiration Point, or Bryce Point.

"Golden light illuminates the hoodoos, enhancing the landscape's varying shades of deep red and orange."

Shivering, we stand waiting for the sun to rise over Bryce Amphitheater. At over 8,000 ft / 2,440 m, it's barely above freezing along the Rim Trail in early spring. The sun peeks over the horizon and an incredible scene begins to unfold. Golden light illuminates the hoodoos, enhancing the landscape's varying shades of deep red and orange. A peacefulness falls across the crowd of onlookers, everyone mesmerized by what they are witnessing. Our frozen toes and fingers quickly warm up as the sun rises higher in the sky, and we capture our final sunrise images. I guess those guidebooks weren't lying when they said sunrise at Bryce Canyon was one of the most beautiful sights you'll ever see.

CANYONLANDS NATIONAL PARK

Wild Landscapes & Ancient History

Canyonlands National Park is best known for its wild landscapes and ancient history. The park has five sections: Island in the Sky, the Needles, the Maze, Horseshoe Canyon Unit, and the Rivers. Most visitors find themselves in the Island in the Sky area, due to its easy access and abundance of short walks and overlooks. The entire mesa top can be toured via a 34 mi / 55 km round-trip scenic drive. Some notable and accessible overlooks include Shaffer Canyon, Green River, Buck Canyon, and Grand View Point.

LOCATION Utah
PARK SIZE 337,598 acres
ICONIC FEATURE Mesa Arch
BEST SEASON Spring and fall
VISIT TIME Best explored in 1-2 days
STAY Camp at Willow Flat Campground, or stay in nearby Moab.

MUST HIKE Mesa Arch, Grand View Point, and Chesler Park Viewpoint trails
PHOTO TIP Green River Overlook, Mesa Arch, and Grand View Point are beautiful photo spots. It can get extremely busy at Mesa Arch for sunrise photography, so be sure to arrive early.

“Wilderness is not a luxury but a necessity of the human spirit, and as vital to our lives as water and good bread.”

– Edward Abbey

It’s 5 a.m. as we step out of our van and begin the short walk to Mesa Arch. The night sky is dark and littered with stars, and the fresh spring air stings our fingers as we follow the path with our headlamps. We arrive at the arch and patiently wait for sunrise, watching stars fade and a glow begin to appear on the horizon. There are about 20 other people besides us when the sun begins to rise, but not even the crowds can dampen what we behold that morning. The sun lights up the underside of Mesa Arch, making it glow as if on fire. Everyone falls silent and we stare in awe at such a wonder.

10

CAPITOL REEF NATIONAL PARK

Apple Pies & Fiery Skies

Capitol Reef National Park is an incredible vista of impressive domes, soaring monoliths, and sandstone cliffs. Home to North America's second largest monocline, the 100 mi / 161 km Waterpocket Fold twists and turns through the park. Visitors can explore this and other geologic wonders by driving the park's scenic roads or getting out on foot for a day hike or camping adventure. Many people also visit Capitol Reef to learn about the area's rich cultural history, including the chance to see ancient petroglyphs and relics of early Mormon settlers. For those willing to brave primitive roads, the Cathedral Valley district is a wonderful place to escape the crowds and get up close and personal with magnificent rock formations.

LOCATION Utah
PARK SIZE 241,904 acres
ICONIC FEATURE Cathedral Valley and the Fruita Rural Historic District
BEST SEASON Spring and fall

VISIT TIME Best explored in 1-2 days
STAY Camp at Fruita Campground in the historic Fruita District, or stay in the various towns near the park.
MUST HIKE Cassidy Arch Trail and Capitol Gorge Trail
PHOTO TIP Explore the Cathedral Valley area, especially the Temples of the Sun and Moon for sunrise and sunset photography.

"Our van, Ruby, rattles along the bumpy roads that lead to the Temple of the Sun and Moon, arriving completely covered in dust."

We stop by the historic Gifford House Store on our way out to Cathedral Valley. Rumor has it they sell the best apple pies in Utah, so naturally we stock up the van and even buy the homemade ice cream to serve with the pastry. Our van, Ruby, rattles along the bumpy roads that lead to the Temple of the Sun and Moon, arriving completely covered in dust. Sunset is approaching rapidly, and we scramble to find a panoramic vantage point to take photos of the huge monoliths. After the sun's last glow fades, we head back to the van, pull out our table, and sample the delicious apple pies. It's one of those pinch-yourself moments... Are we really living this incredible life?!

11

CARLSBAD CAVERNS NATIONAL PARK

A Magical Underground World

Carlsbad Caverns is located in the Chihuahuan Desert, only 35 mi / 56 km from its sister national park, Guadalupe Mountains. Given the close proximity, many visitors choose to explore both national parks in one trip. The main attraction of Carlsbad Caverns National Park is its magical underground world of limestone caves. These 300 limestone chambers are home to magnificent cave formations and can be explored via 30 mi / 48 km of passages. The park runs ranger-led tours and offers self-guided sections of the cave. Amazingly, the deepest chamber reaches 1,037 feet below the surface.

We pull into the parking lot and immediately wonder whether we are in the right place. There is just one building, three trails, and a single road, which is very unlike the other national parks we have visited thus far. We buy our cave tour tickets and are ushered into the elevator to travel some 750 ft / 229 m underground. Our guide takes us from one magnificent chamber to the next, pointing out exquisite cave formations, and at one point he turns off the lights. We stand in complete darkness, not even enough light to see your own hands. It makes sense to us by the end of the tour: Carlsbad Caverns is all about the wonders beneath the surface, not in the desert lands above.

LOCATION New Mexico
PARK SIZE 46,766 acres
ICONIC FEATURE The Big Room cave chamber
BEST SEASON Year round
VISIT TIME Best explored in 1-2 days

STAY There are no lodging options or campgrounds in the park. Stay in nearby towns of White City or Carlsbad.
MUST HIKE King's Palace guided cave tour and the Big Room self-guided walking path
PHOTO TIP Use of tripods is allowed on self-guided trails and is recommended due to the very low light in the underground caves.

12

CHANNEL ISLANDS NATIONAL PARK

Escape Across The Channel

Despite only being 25 mi / 50 km off the coast of Santa Barbara, Channels Islands National Park feels like a world away from the hustle and bustle of everyday life. The park is made up off five islands, all beautiful and unique in their own way: Anacapa, Santa Barbara, Santa Cruz, San Miguel, and Santa Rosa. Channels Islands National Park is only accessible by boat and all areas must be explored on foot or by kayak or boat. Visitors come to the park on day trips and some choose to stay longer to enjoy the plentiful opportunities for hiking, camping, kayaking, swimming, diving, and wildlife observing.

LOCATION California

PARK SIZE 249,561 acres

ICONIC FEATURE The various wildlife, including whales, dolphins, seals, seabirds, and the well-known Santa Cruz island fox

BEST SEASON Year round

VISIT TIME Best explored in 1-2 days

STAY Camp overnight in a primitive campground such as Scorpion Ranch on Santa Cruz Island.

MUST HIKE Inspiration Point on Anacapa Island, Potato Harbor on Santa Cruz Island, or consider taking a kayaking tour.

PHOTO TIP Take a zoom lens to capture wildlife around the islands, consider getting out on the water for marine life encounters, and be sure to witness sunset from a scenic vantage point such as Potato Harbor.

"It's just us and nature... No cars, no sirens, no street lights, Not even a single bar of phone service."

It's Matthew's birthday and we wake in our tent to a beautiful and sunny California day. We celebrate by having a slow morning, cooking breakfast at the campsite, reading our books under a shady tree, and laughing at the tiny island foxes scampering around. In the late afternoon, we hike east along the coast to Cavern Point and continue to Potato Harbor for sunset. We find a quiet spot, sit back, and enjoy the fresh ocean air and island solitude. Seals sun-bake on rocks below us and island foxes cheekily come and say hi. It's just us and nature... No cars, no sirens, no street lights, not even a single bar of phone service.

13

CONGAREE NATIONAL PARK

Escape Into Nature For A Day

Congaree National Park is a slice of nature tucked between cities and suburbia. The park's lush forests and rivers are places where people can connect with the natural world in a peaceful and educational way, making it feel like you are a world away from the realities of everyday life. Interestingly, the park boasts the largest tract of old-growth bottomland hardwood forest remaining in the southeastern United States. There are numerous trails in the park that allow visitors to get up close and personal with these beautiful trees, particularly the Low and High Boardwalk Trails, River Trail, and Oakridge Trail.

The first sign we come across at the Visitor Center is a "mosquito meter". It ranges from "1 - All Clear" to "6 - War Zone". This leaves us wary about what to expect from Congaree. We set off on the High Boardwalk Trail and within minutes encounter a small snake, numerous spiders, sightings of small birds, and a few too many mosquitos. We venture on through the forest past beautiful bald cypress trees, loblolly pines, oaks, maples, and old-growth bottomland hardwood trees. Number markings along the trail correspond with a brochure from the Visitor Center, teaching us about the local vegetation and wildlife, and making the experience feel almost like a scavenger hunt.

LOCATION South Carolina
PARK SIZE 26,276 acres
ICONIC FEATURE Low and High Boardwalk Trails
BEST SEASON Spring and fall
VISIT TIME Can easily be explored in 1 day
STAY Tent camp at Longleaf Campground within the park, or the nearby city of Columbia offers numerous lodging options.
MUST HIKE Low and High Boardwalk Trails and Weston Lake Loop Trail
PHOTO TIP Explore the Boardwalk Trails in early morning or late afternoon for soft, filtered light. Consider taking a seat for 5-10 minutes on one of the numerous benches and see what wildlife come out to say hello.

PHOTOGRAPHING THE PARKS

Tips And Tricks

GEAR

The cameras we used to photograph the national parks were a Sony a7Rii, Sony a9, and a Go Pro Hero 5 Black for this trip. Throughout the trip we frequently reached for three main camera lenses: a 16-35mm (for wide landscapes), 24-70mm (mid-range, most versatile), and a 70-200mm (for capturing wildlife and distant scenery).

TIPS

- Capture images at sunrise and sunset for the best light and to avoid the crowds.
- Use a tripod to stabilize your camera for capturing images in low light and for long exposures (e.g. blurred-looking waterfalls).
- Take self-portraits of yourself and your travel companions by using a tripod and the timer or intervalometer function on your camera.
- Try capturing the stars after dark—many of the parks have incredibly dark and starry skies!
- Use a waterproof camera at the water-based parks to photograph marine life and corals.
- Many of the most picturesque locations require some hiking to get to. If shooting early or late in the day, bring along a headlamp for safely accessing your location in the dark.
- Always follow signs and regulations. A photo isn't worth risking your life for, endangering wildlife, or damaging fragile terrain.
- Make sure you don't just experience the parks through your viewfinder. Be sure to remember to pause, put your camera down, and take in the wonder before you.

14

CRATER LAKE NATIONAL PARK

The Deepest Lake In America

A visitor's first view of Crater Lake is unforgettable. This gem of the Cascades is set within a dormant volcano called Mount Mazama. When it erupted in 5700 B.C., a huge caldera was formed, which eventually filled with rain and snowmelt. This formed Crater Lake, the deepest lake in the United States and what is said to be the cleanest and clearest large body of water in the world. The national park draws large crowds during summer months, with popular activities including scenic drives, hiking, camping, swimming, fishing, and bicycling. Sadly, the area has been hit hard by wildfires in recent years, and smoky conditions are often encountered during the warmer months.

We wake before sunrise with stinging eyes, sore throats, and a dusting of ashfall on the van. Another smoky day in Oregon… the theme of our last few weeks on the West Coast. We pack up and drive to the Visitor Center parking lot, apparently the only people crazy enough to be up at this hour in such conditions. Despite the thick smoke, the lake looks magical as the sun rises, with an almost eerie feeling and not another soul in sight. We explore the rim trail on foot and then drive to various lookouts around the lake, stopping by waterfalls and lush forests as we go. Sadly, we are forced to leave the park a day early due to health warnings, but we know we will return to this beautiful park in the future.

LOCATION Oregon
PARK SIZE 183,224 acres
ICONIC FEATURE View of Crater Lake and Wizard Island from overlooks near the Visitor Center and Crater Lake Lodge
BEST SEASON Late spring through early fall
VISIT TIME Can easily be explored in 1-2 days
STAY Camp at Mazama Campground, or stay in comfort at the historic Crater Lake Lodge.
MUST HIKE Watchman Peak Trail and Cleetwood Cove Trail
PHOTO TIP Capture sunrise over Crater Lake and Wizard Island from the summit of Watchman Peak. The various overlooks near the Visitor Center also provide stunning lake views.

CUYAHOGA VALLEY NATIONAL PARK

History & Beauty All In One

Similar to only a few other parks around the country, Cuyahoga Valley is best known for its rich history as well as its stunning natural beauty. A famous 308 mi / 495 km long waterway – the Ohio & Erie Canal – was built in the Cuyahoga Valley area back in the 1800s. Part of the waterway runs through the national park, allowing visitors to enjoy its history from an adjacent running path, the Towpath Trail, and the popular Cuyahoga Valley Scenic Railroad. The park is open year-round, though it is at its most beautiful in summer and fall when the foliage is lush and vibrant.

LOCATION Ohio
PARK SIZE 33,000 acres
ICONIC FEATURE Ohio & Erie Canal, plus the associated Towpath Trail and Scenic Railroad
BEST SEASON Summer and fall

VISIT TIME Best explored in 1-2 days
STAY Experience staying at a historical inn-like Stanford House or the Inn at Brandywine Falls, both open year-round and inside the park.
MUST HIKE Brandywine Gorge Trail
PHOTO TIP Capture sunrise at Brandywine Falls and sunset at the Ledges, and be sure to check out Everett Road Covered Bridge.

It's early summer and the meadows are brimming with fresh growth and wildlife. We pull our van into the parking lot of the well-known Ledges trailhead. The area is fairytale-like and our senses are instantly delighted as we begin along the trail. As the sun glows through the foliage, we are greeted with the sweet smell of pines and the sounds of birds chirping merrily. We exclaim to each other how peaceful the area feels, given how close we are to the bustling and very nearby reality of suburbia and highways. Sunset from the Ledges does not disappoint, and contentment is the theme of our slow walk back to the van.

"As the sun glows through the foliage, we are greeted with the sweet smell of pines and the sounds of birds chirping merrily."

16

DEATH VALLEY NATIONAL PARK

Otherworldly Landscapes

Death Valley National Park is famous for being the hottest, driest, and lowest region of the United States. Visitors are mesmerized by otherworldly landscapes of sand dunes, salt flats, badlands, lake beds, trickling creeks, and fields of wildflowers. The park is open year-round, though it's advisable to visit during the winter or shoulder seasons due to scorching temperatures over the summer. An eclectic crowd is drawn to Death Valley, including photographers, artists, hikers, bikers, stargazers, birdwatchers, scientists, and road-trippers.

LOCATION California

PARK SIZE 3,400,000 acres

ICONIC FEATURE Badwater Basin and Artist's Drive

BEST SEASON Fall through spring

VISIT TIME Best explored in 1-2 days

STAY Choose somewhere with air-conditioning, like Stovepipe Wells Hotel or a cabin at Panamint Springs Resort.

MUST HIKE Zabriskie Point Overlook and Badlands Loop trails

PHOTO TIP Capture the Mesquite Flat Sand Dunes at sunset and Zabriskie Point at sunrise.

Everything burns as we hike out on the Mesquite Flat Sand Dunes for sunset. We slowly climb the hot sand and sink calf-deep with every step, our bodies and lungs screaming from the effort. Finally, we make it to the top of a large dune, throw down our packs, and fall into the sand to catch our breath. Stillness envelops us as we sit in solitude, watching golden light hitting the windswept crests. Sunset is glorious and pink but quickly overshadowed, for what follows afterwards will forever be etched in our minds. The full moon rises over the sand dunes and fills the area with an unfathomable glimmer. The moonlight guides us back to our car and leaves us buzzing for hours.

"Stillness envelops us as we sit in solitude, watching golden light hitting the windswept crests."

DENALI NATIONAL PARK

Where The Wild Things Are

Denali National Park is world-famous for its natural beauty, plentiful wildlife, and sheer size. The park was named after its crowning jewel: Mount Denali (formerly Mount McKinley), standing at 20,320 ft / 6,194 m above sea level. Exploring Denali can be challenging due to restrictions on access by private vehicles in the majority of the park. Visitors can take a concessioner-operated bus along the entire 92 mi / 148 km main park road, which stops at campsites and various areas of interest along the way. Bus drivers and rangers provide narration on the park's history and iconic views and will stop for wildlife viewings.

LOCATION Alaska
PARK SIZE 6,075,030 acres
ICONIC FEATURE Mount Denali (formerly Mount McKinley)
BEST SEASON Summer
VISIT TIME Highlights in 1-2 days, or best explored in 3-4 days
STAY Camp at one of the many scenic park-run campgrounds, such as Wonder Lake, Teklanika River, and Savage River Campground.

MUST HIKE Savage River Loop Trail, or consider taking a backcountry hiking and camping adventure.
PHOTO TIP Take a ranger-led bus tour for opportunities to photograph wildlife, capture images of Mount Denali from the Eielson Visitor Center, or consider a flightseeing tour over the park for epic aerial views.

Denali National Park and Preserve

It's day 3 and we have yet to glimpse Mount Denali. We are told this weather is fairly typical for late August, but the relentless drizzle is starting to take its toll. We are beginning to run out of reading material, have drunk almost all of our hot chocolate, and are keenly aware that the inside of our tent is distinctly damp. We board the bus back toward civilization and we are hopeful, as the clouds appear to be lifting. Our bus driver points out grizzly bears, caribou, and moose as we amble along the bumpy road, everyone scrambling for their cameras. The weather finally clears enough for us to take in a brief view of Denali's famed peak, and what a sight it is!

"The weather finally clears enough for us to take in a brief view of Denali's famed peak, and what a sight it is!"

18

DRY TORTUGAS NATIONAL PARK

A Water Lover's Paradise

Dry Tortugas is not what people usually think of when considering America's national parks. Located 70 mi / 113 km off the coast of Key West, the park is 99% water, while the remaining 1% is made up of seven major islands. Most visitors come to Dry Tortugas to explore the island known as Garden Key and the impressive Fort Jefferson. Private water vessels are allowed in the park, though most visitors opt to take a day tour on the park service ferry, the Yankee Freedom III, which operates out of Key West. Popular things to do in the park include snorkeling, diving, sunbathing, swimming, stand-up paddleboarding, kayaking, and touring Fort Jefferson.

LOCATION Florida
PARK SIZE 64,701 acres
ICONIC FEATURE Fort Jefferson on Garden Key
BEST SEASON Year round
VISIT TIME Best explored in 1-2 days
STAY Primitive camp on Garden Key, or stay in town back in Key West.

MUST HIKE Take a walking tour of Fort Jefferson (guided or unguided), and snorkel the many 'water trails' around Garden Key.
PHOTO TIP Photograph the colorful reef life, marine life, and corals by packing a waterproof camera, such as a GoPro, or by picking up a waterproof case for your camera.

"Before this trip, we had no idea such a wonder existed off the coast of Florida."

Our captain comes on over the loudspeaker, informing us that we will be arriving at Garden Key soon. Fort Jefferson comes into view, perched grandly on its white sand island and surrounded by pristine turquoise water. We disembark and head straight for the fort's rooftop, where we are treated to 360-degree ocean views and an aerial perspective of the impressive moat running around the island. We watch pelicans fish and try to spot the elusive friendly crocodile that is said to be an island local. Before long, we find ourselves running into the refreshing water for a turn snorkeling the coral reefs. Before this trip, we had no idea such a wonder existed off the coast of Florida.

19

EVERGLADES NATIONAL PARK

The River Of Grass

Everglades National Park is world-famous for its unique plethora of wildlife. With a huge landmass to explore, the park has four main entrances: Shark Valley and Gulf Coast in the north, and Royal Palm and Flamingo in the south. Shark Valley and Royal Palm are the two most popular sections, offering interpretive trails, viewing decks, and an abundance of beautiful flora and fauna. The majority of visitors explore the park during the dry season (November to March) due to more bearable temperatures, fewer bugs, and the largest variety of wading birds and their predators.

LOCATION Florida

PARK SIZE 1,508,538 acres

ICONIC FEATURE Unique wildlife, such as alligators and crocodiles

BEST SEASON Winter

VISIT TIME Best explored in 1-2 days

STAY The park has three main campgrounds, backcountry camping options, and ample accommodations in towns bordering the park.

MUST HIKE Anhinga Trail and Gumbo Limbo Trail

PHOTO TIP Get out on the trails at sunrise for a better chance to spot wildlife, plus the soft golden light and calm waters that provide a perfect scene for photographs.

"There are no other Everglades in the world. They are, they have always been, one of the unique regions of the earth, remote, never wholly known. Nothing anywhere else is like them..."

– Marjory Stoneman Douglas

Every corner we take leads to another wildlife encounter. Huge alligators swim only steps away, grunting and roaring to attract mates. Baby alligators sunbathe right next to the path, and we warily move on in case their mother makes an appearance. Wading birds explore the shallow river next to us, going about their business as if we aren't there. All of a sudden, a bird flies out of the marsh next to us, holding a small snake in its mouth. The snake struggles to get free as the bird soars away. We laugh out loud and exclaim to each other just how wild the Everglades truly are.

GREATEST PARK LODGES & CAMP GROUNDS

Top Places To Stay

Old Faithful Inn, **YELLOWSTONE**
Half Dome Village, **YOSEMITE**
Jenny Lake Campground, **GRAND TETON**
Crater Lake Lodge, **CRATER LAKE**
Many Glacier Lodge & Campground, **GLACIER**
Brooks Falls Campground, **KATMAI**
Wonder Lake Campground, **DENALI**
Hope Creek Campground, **LAKE CLARK**
Glacier Bay Lodge & Campground, **GLACIER BAY**
Paradise Inn, **MOUNT RAINIER**
Jumbo Rocks Campground, **JOSHUA TREE**
Exit Glacier Campground, **KENAI FJORDS**
Moraine Park Campground, **ROCKY MOUNTAIN**
Big Meadows Lodge & Campground, **SHENANDOAH**
Kennicott Glacier Lodge, **WRANGELL-ST. ELIAS**

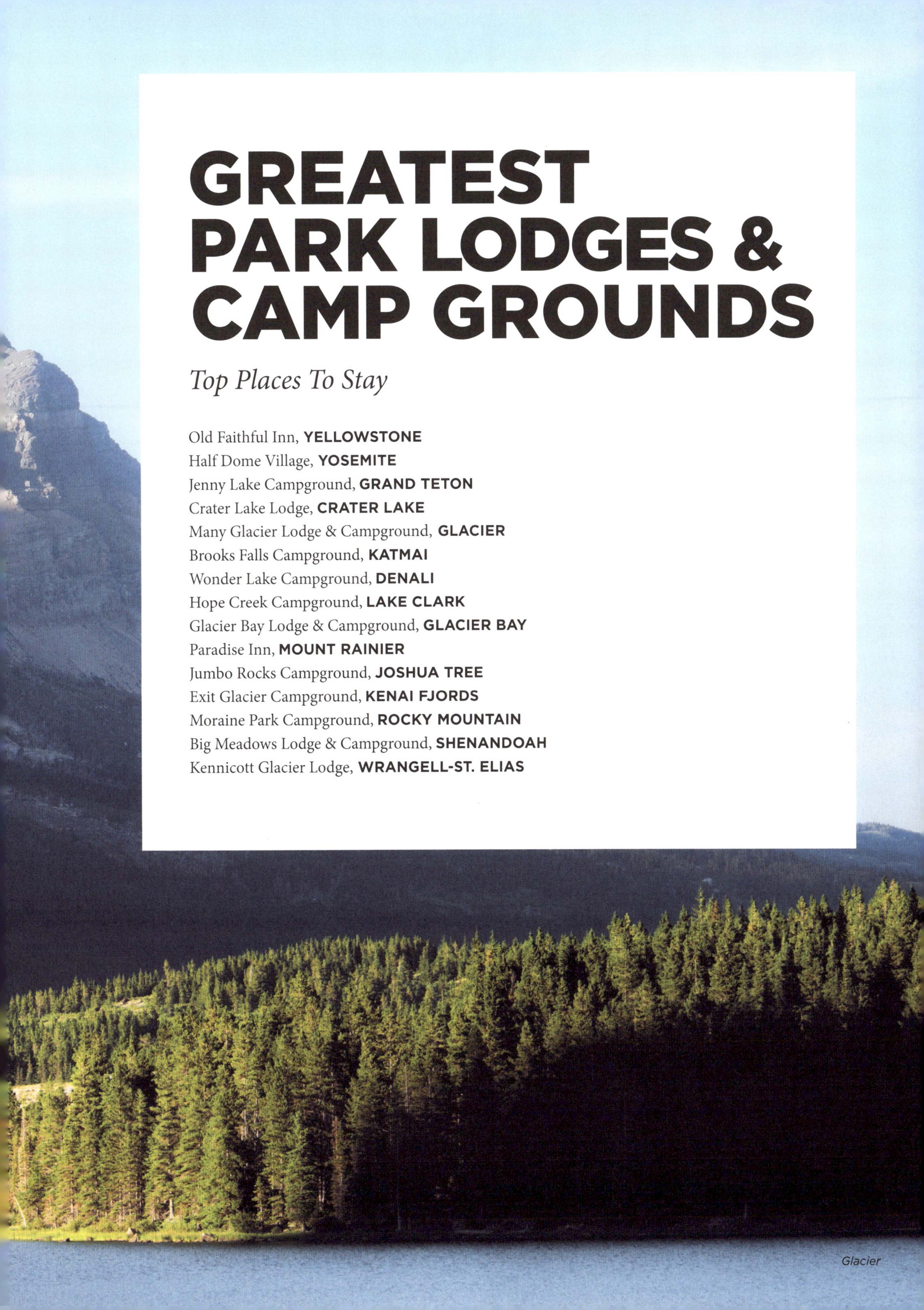

Glacier

20

GATES OF THE ARCTIC NATIONAL PARK

A Rugged Slice Of Natural Beauty

There aren't many places left on earth that are as wild as Gates of the Arctic National Park. Located within the Arctic Circle, the park is extremely remote and does not have any roads, maintained trails, or facilities of any kind. Visitors are faced with a choice of plane, foot, or watercraft to access the park, and many fly into the small town of Bettles to begin their journey. The Arrigetch Peaks are arguably the most famous section of the park. Adventure seekers come from all over the world to hike the jaw-dropping valleys, climb jagged granite spires, and packraft down the nearby Alatna River.

LOCATION Alaska
PARK SIZE 8,472,506 acres
ICONIC FEATURE Arrigetch Peaks and the Alatna River
BEST SEASON Summer
VISIT TIME Flightseeing tour in 1 day, or ideally explored in 7+ days on a backcountry trek
STAY Camp in the backcountry, or stay in the nearby town of Bettles.
MUST HIKE Arrigetch Peaks backpacking trip
PHOTO TIP Bring lots of batteries, because there are endless opportunities to capture mountain peaks, rivers, wildlife, and foliage.

Fear. Excitement. Second-guessing. These are just a few of the feelings running through our minds as we board the float plane. Goodbye civilization… we will reconnect in ten days. We have no idea of the adventure that is ahead of us. Not yet molded by the beauty of the Arrigetch, the treacherous miles covered, the grizzly bear and wolf encounters, the penetrating silence of the wilderness, and the fickleness of Mother Nature. Little do we know how our lives will change as we step into the isolated wonderland that is Gates of the Arctic.

"Little do we know how our lives will change as we step into the isolated wonderland that is Gates of the Arctic."

21

GLACIER BAY NATIONAL PARK

Sea To Summit Beauty

Glacier Bay National Park is a nature lover's dream. Home to beautiful mountains, famous glaciers, an abundance of wildlife, cultural history, and lush rainforest, it's not hard to see why. The park can be accessed by water or air, with most visitors touring Glacier Bay on a cruise ship or flying into nearby Gustavas. Bartlett Cove is the only developed area in the park, which is where you can find the Visitor Center, lodge, boat tours, hiking trails, Huna Tlingit exhibits, a public boat dock, sea kayak rentals, and a walk-in campground. Many visitors also opt to take multi-day sea-kayaking adventures around Glacier Bay, with guided and self-guided options available.

LOCATION Alaska

PARK SIZE 3,300,000 acres

ICONIC FEATURE Margerie and Johns Hopkins tidewater glaciers

BEST SEASON Summer

VISIT TIME Highlights in 1-2 days, or best explored in 3-4 days

STAY Camp at walk-in Bartlett Cove Campground, or stay in comfort at the Glacier Bay Lodge.

MUST HIKE Forest Loop and Bartlett River trails

PHOTO TIP Take a boat tour and photograph glaciers, explore the trails and capture the lush forest, and head out on a kayak to get up close and personal with marine life.

It hasn't stopped raining since we arrived. Not a heavy downpour, just a seemingly constant mist and layer of fog. We spent the day out on a boat tour, witnessing glaciers calving, spotting whales and bald eagles, and photographing bears on the distant shoreline. It's now time to explore the many trails leading from Bartlett Cove. As we hike into the temperate rainforest, we are instantly greeted by evergreen trees, moss-covered logs, and the smell of fresh rain. It isn't long before one of us spots some fresh bear tracks in the muddy soil. We cautiously proceed down the trail, but soon turn around when it becomes apparent the tracks are from a mother and her cubs. Best to let them be; there are plenty more trails to be explored.

"From the summit to sea, Glacier Bay's wildness is remote, dynamic, and intact."

– National Park Service

22

GLACIER NATIONAL PARK

A Gem Of The Park System

Simply put, Glacier National Park is one of the most beautiful places on earth. Best known for its turquoise lakes, majestic mountains, picturesque scenic drives, and abundant wildlife, Glacier has it all. The most visited sections of the park include Apgar/Lake McDonald, St. Mary, Two Medicine, and the Many Glacier Area, though some visitors instead choose to escape the crowds and explore the park's beautiful wilderness areas. Glacier's crowning glory is undoubtedly the Going-to-the-Sun Road, a scenic drive that travels 53 mi / 85 km into the heart of the park, providing jaw-dropping scenery at every bend.

LOCATION Montana

PARK SIZE 1,012,837 acres

ICONIC FEATURE Going-to-the-Sun Road

BEST SEASON Summer

VISIT TIME Highlights in 1-2 days, or best explored in 4-6 days

STAY Camp at various established campgrounds in the park, such as Fish Creek, St. Mary, Apgar Glacier, and Many Glacier, or stay at one of the park's historic lodges, such as Lake McDonald Lodge.

MUST HIKE Avalanche Lake and Iceberg Lake trails

PHOTO TIP Glacier has seemingly endless photo locations. Some of the best include the Many Glacier Area at sunrise, and the Going-to-the-Sun Road and Lake McDonald at sunset.

EAGLE

"Far away in Montana, hidden from the view by clustering mountain peaks, lies an unmapped northwestern corner – the Crown of the Continent. Here is a land of striking scenery."

– George Bird Grinnell

It's mid-afternoon and we set off toward Iceberg Lake, some 5 mi / 8 km into the backcountry. This year has seen a super-bloom of bear grass and the mountainsides surrounding us are covered with thousands of whitish-yellow blossoms. Finally, we arrive at the lake. Unsurprisingly, it's dotted with chunks of ice and looks to be absolutely freezing. We aren't brave enough to take a dip, so instead we capture a bunch of photos, enjoy a snack with a view, and start our hike back to the van. Before we know it, the sun goes down and the forest becomes eerily quiet. We proceed to yell "hey bear!" for the next 5 miles and have a close encounter with a dazed deer (which we initially thought was a mountain lion). This place is wild.

23

GRAND CANYON NATIONAL PARK

The Grandest Of Canyons

Grand Canyon National Park is world famous for its dramatic landscapes, sheer size, and unparalleled beauty. The South and North Rims of the Grand Canyon offer maintained roads, lodging, camping, and numerous opportunities for adventure, with the popular West Rim actually lying outside of the park boundaries. Each year, most visitors find themselves along the South Rim due to its accessibility and iconic views. Despite drawing large crowds, it is easy to escape the masses and explore the wilderness of the Grand Canyon on foot. One of the biggest adventures of them all is hiking the famed Rim-to-Rim Trail, covering a length of 23.5 mi / 37.8 km and an elevation change of 10,710 ft / 3,265 m (hiked North to South).

LOCATION Arizona
PARK SIZE 1,217,403 acres
ICONIC FEATURE Mather Point on the South Rim
BEST SEASON Spring and fall
VISIT TIME Highlights in 1-2 days, or best explored in 3-5 days
STAY The South and North Rims have both camping and lodging options.

MUST HIKE Explore Kaibab Trail on the South Rim, where hikers can take the trail as far as their physical fitness allows, right down to the Colorado River if they wish.
PHOTO TIP The South Rim offers countless photogenic viewpoints. Sunrise is best captured from Mather Point, and sunset is a magical sight from Hopi Point and Mojave Point.

"In the Grand Canyon, Arizona has a natural wonder which is in kind absolutely unparalleled throughout the rest of the world."

– *Theodore Roosevelt*

We set off in the late afternoon, though the sun burns our skin as if it's still midday. The Kaibab trail leads us down the canyon and we can't help but stop every few minutes to take in the seemingly never-ending epic views. We decide to end our descent at Skeleton Point for sunset. As cliché as it sounds, it simply cannot be captured in a photograph or described in words. Similarly, the peacefulness is beyond anything we had imagined such a busy park would offer us. It really is just us and the mighty canyon walls. The sun's last glow fades as we put on our head lamps and begin the upwards journey back to the van.

24

GRAND TETON NATIONAL PARK

Jagged Peaks & Alpine Lakes

Grand Teton National Park is a gem of the Rockies and shouldn't be overlooked by visitors exploring its sister park, Yellowstone. Grand Teton is home to some of the world's most majestic mountain vistas, abundant wildlife, scenic hikes, and seemingly endless sights to see. Grand Teton is open year-round and each season brings a new feel to the park. Winter results in gorgeous snow-covered peaks and temperatures as low as -60 F°/ -51 C°, fall is the perfect time to witness colorful foliage, spring brings new life and lush meadows, and summer is the best time for hiking and exploring in the backcountry.

LOCATION Wyoming
PARK SIZE 310,000 acres
ICONIC FEATURE The Grand Teton (13,770 ft; 4,197 m)
BEST SEASON Summer and fall

VISIT TIME Highlights in 1-2 days, or best explored in 4-5 days
STAY Camp at Jenny Lake for incredible views, or in nearby Jackson Hole.
MUST HIKE Cascade Canyon Trail to Solitude Lake
PHOTO TIP Capture the sunrise glow along the Teton Range from the Black Tail Ponds lookout or Schwabacher Landing.

"There's nothing quite like the feeling of witnessing the Teton Mountain Range for the first time. It's a view we could never tire of and one we will continue to seek out season after season, year after year."

We park our van on a hillside overlooking the mountains. It's after dark and the sky is blanketed with stars. We settle in for the night and set our alarms for sunrise. The next morning, we groggily wake and set about opening the curtains. I catch a glimpse of a pink alpine glow kissing the Grand Teton and squeal in awe. We open up the back of the van and proceed to watch Mother Nature's beauty unfold until the sun peeks over the mountainside. We eat breakfast, capture some images and write in our journal. It's moments like these that we will cherish forever.

25

GREAT BASIN NATIONAL PARK

Ancient Trees, Peaks, & Caves

Great Basin is one of the least visited, most secluded, and most underrated national parks in the country. Often referred to as "Nevada's best-kept secret," Great Basin is home to what many scientists say is the world's oldest living organism: the bristlecone pine. The park is also famous for its impressive mountain peaks and a unique cave system filled with intricate formations. The park is open year-round, though Wheeler Peak Scenic Drive is partially closed in winter due to the snow pack.

LOCATION Nevada
PARK SIZE 77,180 acres
ICONIC FEATURE Bristlecone pine
BEST SEASON Summer
VISIT TIME Highlights in 1-2 days, or best explored in 2-3 days
STAY Camp at the Wheeler Peak Campground for beautiful views and the experience of sleeping at high altitude.
MUST HIKE Bristlecone Trail
PHOTO TIP Great Basin is known for its deep, starry skies, so perfect for capturing unique night-time images with the stars, bristlecone pines, and mountain peaks.

"Our fingers might be numb, but our hearts are full from experiencing one of the earth's most extraordinary creations."

The wind rips at our jackets and snow starts to fall lightly around us. It feels insignificant to what we are witnessing, for in front of us stands 3,000 to 4,000-year-old ancient bristlecone pines. These trees have battled extreme conditions such as freezing temperatures, buckling winds, and high elevation. It is mesmerizing to observe their thick, twisted trunks and think that some have grown to be 5,000 years old. Our fingers might be numb, but our hearts are full from experiencing one of the earth's most extraordinary creations.

Grand Teton

VAN LIFE TIPS

Living On The Road

For our seven-month-long road trip, we lived in a 1988 Westfalia Vanagon, which was lent to us by our friends at Go Westy. 'Ruby' truly became our home on wheels during those months, and we sure did learn a thing or two about van life along the way! Keep these tips in mind when planning your own camper van or RV road trip.

- Use all the space in the van as efficiently as possible, and store your most-used items in easy-to-access locations.
- Save money by camping/parking overnight for free on Bureau of Land Management (BLM) land just outside many of the national parks.
- Make a road trip playlist filled with good tunes and podcasts for those long drives.
- Invest in a cooler or electric fridge to store fresh food, which allows for healthier meals. Make sure you have a way to keep it charged—a second battery and/or solar panels work great.
- Live as minimally as possible when it comes to clothing, shoes, dishware, etc. This will allow for a clutter-free space and an overall better experience. Merino wool clothing is great, as it doesn't need to be washed as often!
- Create a cosy feeling in the van so that it feels more like home. Use twinkle lights, curtains, blankets, pillows, and photos to make it your own space.
- Have some routines that help you feel grounded when constantly moving from place to place. This might include daily journaling, reading, having a quiet cup of tea, or exercising.
- Have a designated place for everything in the van, so things don't get too messy!
- Set yourself up to succeed by planning out personalized ways to have fun and stay healthy before taking your van trip.
- Set up a tablet or laptop and treat yourself to a van "movie night". You can find inventive ways to mount this, depending on the layout of your van.
- Learn some basic car repair skills for unexpected breakdowns in the middle of nowhere!

26

GREAT SAND DUNES NATIONAL PARK

Tallest Dunes In North America

Located only 4 hours south of Denver, Great Sand Dunes National Park is one of Colorado's most unexpected natural wonders. Picture this: America's tallest sand dunes nestled against huge 13,000 ft / 4,000 m+ mountain peaks... This park is magnificently wild. Great Sand Dunes National Park has three unique ecosystems – alpine desert, grassland, and forest – with each providing a range of activities for visitors to immerse themselves in. Hiking, camping, sand-boarding/sledding, and cooling off in the Medano Creek are popular things to do. Be mindful that the park experiences extreme heat in summer and bitter cold in winter, so plan accordingly.

LOCATION Colorado
PARK SIZE 149,137 acres
ICONIC FEATURE The Great Sand Dunes themselves
BEST SEASON Late spring and early fall
VISIT TIME Best explored in 1-2 days

STAY Backcountry camp out on the dunes, or stay at Piñon Flats Campground.
MUST HIKE The tallest dunes, Star Dune and High Dune
PHOTO TIP Get out on the dunes at sunset for golden light, and consider staying out after dark to photograph some of the starriest skies in the country.

"We yelled to each other through the wind, our voices getting lost as sand pelted against us, stinging our faces and filling our eyes."

Sand everywhere. In our pockets, socks, bags, eyes, nostrils, mouths, hair... Getting stuck in a storm on a 700 ft / 213 m sand dune will do that. The storm rolled in quickly, bringing wind gusts that threatened to knock us over, a sky filled with sand, and eventually snowfall. We yelled to each other through the wind, our voices getting lost as sand pelted against us, stinging our faces and filling our eyes. Shielding our cameras, we ran, tumbled, and fell down the dunes toward our van, laughing at how ridiculous the scene was. As always, nature won and left us humbled by its magnificent force.

27

GREAT SMOKY MOUNTAINS NATIONAL PARK

America's Most Visited National Park

Great Smoky Mountains National Park sprawls across western North Carolina and eastern Tennessee. The Smokies and its associated scenic parkway are part of the Appalachian Mountains, with 72 mi / 116 km of the world-famous Appalachian Trail running right through the park. Every year, Great Smoky Mountains continues to receive the most visitors of any national park in the country (11,338,893 in 2017), and it's easy to see why when you find yourself exploring its wonders. Popular things to do in the park include hiking, camping, photography, wildlife viewing, and driving its many scenic roads.

LOCATION Tennessee and North Carolina
PARK SIZE 522,427 acres
ICONIC FEATURE Cades Cove
BEST SEASON Spring and fall
VISIT TIME Highlights in 1-2 days, or best explored in 3-4 days

STAY Camp in one of the various park campgrounds, or stay in the nearby town of Gatlinburg.
MUST HIKE Alum Cave and Clingmans Dome trails
PHOTO TIP Capture morning light around Cades Cove, sunrise at Oconaluftee Overlook, and sunset at Clingmans Dome.

We both have head colds, probably from the long travel days and change of season. Sniffling, we pull ourselves out of bed and set off in the van toward Cades Cove. Our sore throats are quickly forgotten when we witness the low-lying fog and golden light illuminating the meadows along the scenic drive. Countless white-tailed deer frolic across the road, and we soon spot a black bear in the distance. We spend hours spotting wildlife, taking in the mountain views, and exploring old homesteads. The whole time, we are absolutely in awe of the valley's tucked-away beauty. It will turn out to be one of the best mornings of our entire road trip.

"There are trees here that stood before our forefathers ever came to this continent; there are brooks that still run as clear as the day the first pioneer cupped his hand and drank from them."

– President Franklin D. Roosevelt

28

GUADALUPE MOUNTAINS NATIONAL PARK

The Wild West

Guadalupe Mountains National Park is home to the tallest point in Texas, fascinating natural and culture history, and unique desert landscapes. Best of all, the park is known for its low visitor numbers and year-round accessibility. Located some 35 mi / 56 km from sister park Carlsbad Caverns, these southern gems were once a reef growing beneath the waters of an ancient inland sea. In modern times, visitors are now treated to impressive mountain peaks, dramatically contoured canyons, and hardy desert foliage and wildlife. The park is also home to archeological evidence suggesting that humans have been living in the area for over 10,000 years.

It's early morning and our last day to explore the Guadalupe Mountains. We set off down the Smith Spring Trail not long after sunrise, hoping to beat the hottest part of the day. The rugged desert trail quickly turns into grassy slopes and before we know it, we find ourselves in a patch of oak woodland. It's a sheltered oasis filled with small pools draped in ferns and surrounded by mossy rocks. We find an old log to sit on and take a minute to enjoy the sound of the trickling stream, hoping to catch a glimpse of some wildlife. Having received our nature fix for the day, we head back to the van and onward to our next park.

LOCATION Texas
PARK SIZE 86,416 acres
ICONIC FEATURE Guadalupe Peak (8,751 ft / 2,667 m)
BEST SEASON Year round
VISIT TIME Best explored in 1-2 days
STAY Camp at Pine Springs Campground, or stay in nearby Dell City, Texas or Whites City, New Mexico.

MUST HIKE Smith Spring Trail for a relatively easy desert walk, or summit Guadalupe Peak if you're after a much bigger adventure.
PHOTO TIP Get out on the trails at sunset and capture golden light hitting the Guadalupe Mountains. Pullouts on Highway 62 / Highway 180 also provide panoramic mountain views.

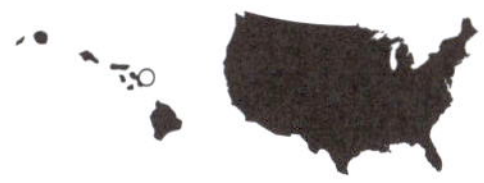

29

HALEAKALĀ NATIONAL PARK

House Of The Sun

Haleakalā National Park is best known for its dramatic views, unique ecosystems, and volcanic history. Split into three main sections – the Summit, Kīpahulu, and Wilderness Districts – there really is something for everyone to enjoy in the park. The Summit District is where visitors can experience the summit of the Haleakalā volcano, impressive landscapes, and rare plants and wildlife. The Kīpahulu District is home to lush rainforests, waterfalls, and beautiful ocean vistas. The Haleakalā Wilderness Area is rich with hiking opportunities, yet extremely barren and unforgiving.

LOCATION Maui, Islands of Hawai'i

PARK SIZE 33,265 acres

ICONIC FEATURE Sunrise or sunset view from the summit of Haleakalā (10,023 ft / 3,055 m)

BEST SEASON Year round

VISIT TIME Best explored in 1-2 days

STAY Camp at Hosmer Grove or Kīpahulu Campground, or stay in nearby towns such as Hāna or Kula.

MUST HIKE Pīpīwai Trail in the Kīpahulu District

PHOTO TIP Capture magnificent sunrise or sunset views from the summit of Haleakalā, and lush bamboo forests along the Pīpīwai Trail. The nearby Road to Hāna also has countless photogenic waterfalls and beaches.

It has been raining all day, that thick, tropical rain that leaves you soaked after a second of being out in it. With only one day left on Maui, we know a trip to the summit of Haleakalā is a must, even in this weather. So off we set, driving through the storm and praying for it to be clear at the top of the volcano. Miraculously, we round a bend in the road just after the visitor center and pop completely out of the clouds. We pull into the first lookout and witness an incredible sight, for we are standing above a 360-degree view of clouds. The golden sunset light proceeds to turn everything to fire, burning orange across the sky and creating a scene like no other.

"No place can prepare you for the experience and feelings you will have on the summit of Haleakalā volcano."

– *National Park Service*

30

HAWAI'I VOLCANOES NATIONAL PARK

Volatile & Ever-changing

Hawai'i Volcanoes National Park has a fiery reputation and history of geothermal activity. The park's landscape is constantly changing due to lava flow and resurfacing from two active volcanoes: Mauna Loa and Kīlauea. Hawai'i Volcanoes' main section can be found in nearby Kīlauea Visitor Center, Jagger Museum, and Crater Rim Drive. Leading from Crater Rim Drive, Chain of Craters Road is a 19 mi / 30 km scenic drive that leads visitors some 3,700 ft / 1,128 m down to the ocean's edge. Sights such as the Hōlei Sea Arch, Devil's Throat, and the Pu'u Loa Petroglyphs are popular points to stop along the way.

Most people have seen lava in movies, or even watched scenes on TV as it engulfed houses and flowed into the ocean off Hawai'i. Not even this could prepare us for seeing it in real life. The lava gave off a searing heat as it broke the surface, leaving us sweating despite the cool night breeze. We stood there watching in awe as it bubbled up from the center of the earth, almost within touching distance before us. Other than the occasional cracking and popping, there was just silence out there on the lava fields. In that moment, it was just us, the stars, and one of Earth's greatest wonders.

LOCATION Big Island, Islands of Hawai'i
PARK SIZE 323,431 acres
ICONIC FEATURE Kīlauea Caldera and Halema'uma'u Crater
BEST SEASON Year round

*Note: Kīlauea Volcano experienced a series of eruptions during early to mid-2018, resulting in a changed landscape and closures compared to when we visited in 2017. These photographs and information are based on our visit; more recent updates can be found via the National Park Service.

VISIT TIME Best explored in 1-2 days
STAY Camp at Nāmakanipaio Campground, or stay in the nearby town of Volcano.
MUST HIKE Thurston Lava Tube Trail, or (when open) hike to overlooks of active lava flow at the end of Chain of Craters Road or Kalapana.
PHOTO TIP Capture lava activity after sunset over Halema'uma'u Crater, where explosive red magma bursts with life under a blanket of stars.

MASSAGE
EXIT

HOT SPRINGS NATIONAL PARK

The American Spa

When you think of a national park, you probably don't envision a vibrant southern town and historic bathhouses. Most famous for its therapeutic waters, Hot Springs was the earliest park unit in the country to have been protected under the National Park Service. The park's best-known feature is Bathhouse Row: a street lined with historic bathhouses and a picturesque Visitor Center. Back in the 1920s and '30s, people came from all over to rejuvenate in one of the many bathhouses, including famous athletes, presidents, and Hollywood stars. The park also offers nature lovers a place of sanctuary, with various walking trails, lookouts, and campsites.

LOCATION Arkansas
PARK SIZE 5,550 acres
ICONIC FEATURE Bathhouse Row
BEST SEASON Spring and fall
VISIT TIME Best explored in 1-2 days
STAY Camp by the river at Gulpha Gorge Campground, or stay in one of the many lodging options in the town of Hot Springs.

MUST HIKE Mountain Top Trail, plus stroll along Bathhouse Row, and take a tour of Fordyce Bathhouse.
PHOTO TIP Head up the Hot Spring Mountain Lookout Tower for sunset to capture 360-degree views over the lush local mountains and historic buildings.

Here goes! I am trying a traditional spa treatment at Buckstaff Bathhouse and have no idea what to expect… My bath attendant tells me to strip off and proceeds to wrap me in a thin sheet. She ushers me to a room with ancient-looking bathtubs and requests that I get in, lie down, and relax. Ten minutes later, she is back to rigorously scrub my back and feet… "This is getting weird," I think to myself. We move to a guillotine-like steam chamber and I politely decline that part of the treatment. Next is a table where steaming hot blankets are placed all over my body. Onwards to a sitz tub, where scalding hot water feels like it's burning my behind. Lastly, it's into a cooling needle shower before being wrapped back in my sheet. What an incredibly odd experience that was.

"There must be quite a few things a hot bath won't cure, but I don't know many of them."

– Sylvia Plath

GYMNASIUM

MOST SCENIC PARK HIKING TRAILS

Get Out & Explore

It seems like there are an infinite number of incredible hikes within the national parks. It was challenging to narrow down our list of the top scenic hiking trails, but we did our best! Though some of the trails listed below can be quite busy, we feel they are still worth braving the crowds.

Queens Garden and Navajo Loop – **BRYCE CANYON**
Trappers Peak – **NORTH CASCADES**
Clouds Rest – **YOSEMITE**
Harding Icefield – **KENAI FJORDS**
Cascade Canyon – **GRAND TETON**
Tolmie Peak – **MOUNT RAINIER**
Old Rag Mountain – **SHENANDOAH**
Observation Point – **ZION**
Mesquite Sand Dunes – **DEATH VALLEY**
Kaibab Trail – **GRAND CANYON**
Cinder Cone Trail – **LASSEN VOLCANIC**
Bristlecone Trail – **GREAT BASIN**
Boy Scout Trail – **REDWOOD**
Santa Elena Canyon – **BIG BEND**
Delicate Arch – **ARCHES**
Grinnell Glacier – **GLACIER**
Chasm Lake – **ROCKY MOUNTAIN**
Mist Trail – **YOSEMITE**
Big Trees Trail – **SEQUOIA**
Upper Geyser Basin – **YELLOWSTONE**

Grand Teton

32

ISLE ROYALE NATIONAL PARK

A Camper's Paradise

Isle Royale National Park is a wildly beautiful place located on an island in the middle of Lake Superior. It's statistically one of the least-visited national parks in the country, though said to be the most revisited. Adventure lovers come to Isle Royale to camp, kayak, and traverse the rugged landscape. The only means of transportation in the park is by foot, kayak, boat, or seaplane, making the island extremely peaceful and undeveloped. Some visitors choose to explore the island on a day-trip from Copper Harbor, Houghton, or Grand Portage, though it's recommended to stay longer for a more in-depth experience.

It has been barely 15 minutes when we encounter our first moose on the trail. Startled, it snorts and quickly trots away, leaving us to continue along to our first backcountry campsite. We encounter two other hikers and one ranger that entire day, confirming what we had been told about Isle Royale's beauty in getting off the beaten path. Lane Cove is where we find ourselves that night, settled along the shore of Lake Superior and offering views of Canada in the distance. We cook dinner, watch a golden sunset, and call it a night. The gentle sound of waves lapping against the shore wakes us in the morning. We begin to pack up camp for another day exploring this wondrous island.

LOCATION Michigan
PARK SIZE 571,790 acres
ICONIC FEATURE Mount Ojibway and the Greenstone Ridge Trail
BEST SEASON Summer
VISIT TIME Highlights in 1 day, or best explored in 3-5 days
STAY Rock Harbor Lodge or, at one of the many backcountry campsites

MUST HIKE Stoll Trail (day hike), or take a 3 to 4-day backpacking trip.

PHOTO TIP Given Isle Royale's position on Lake Superior, sunrise is best captured on the southeast side of the island, and sunset on the northwest side. The Mount Ojibway lookout tower is a great spot for sunrise or sunset photography.

33

JOSHUA TREE NATIONAL PARK

A Desert Wonderland

Joshua Tree is a relatively small yet popular national park, best known for its accessible camping, short trails, clear night skies, and of course, Joshua trees. The park can be accessed via three entrances: west (Joshua Tree Village), north (Twentynine Palms), and south (Cottonwood Spring). The west and north entrances have more services in terms of accommodation and restaurants, compared to the south entrance. Popular visitor activities include hiking, camping, rock climbing, biking, and photography.

LOCATION California
PARK SIZE 789,866 acres
ICONIC FEATURE Desert flora and rock formations
BEST SEASON Spring and fall
VISIT TIME Highlights in 1 day, or best explored in 2-3 days
STAY Camp at White Tank or Jumbo Rocks Campground.

MUST HIKE Arch Rock Nature Trail and Cholla Cactus Garden Trail
PHOTO TIP Night photography is very popular in Joshua Tree because of the limited light pollution and clear skies. Shoot before moonrise or during a new moon for the best views of the Milky Way and other stars.

It's pitch black as we pull the van into our camping spot. The sky is blanketed with stars and the Milky Way is just visible. We set our alarm for sunrise and drift off to sleep. The morning brings a soft glow over the desert. We scramble for our cameras and begin traversing nearby rocks to find the best vantage point. A coyote yips in the distance as the sun peeks over the horizon, lighting up Joshua trees and creating a soft hue on the rocks around us. We begin to hear others waking in the campground, but for now it's just us and the morning stillness.

"A coyote yips in the distance as the sun peeks over the horizon, lighting up Joshua trees and creating a soft hue on the rocks around us."

34

KATMAI NATIONAL PARK & PRESERVE

Bear Country

Located in a remote region of southern Alaska, Katmai is best known for its volcanic activity and North America's largest population of protected brown bears. Visitors can access the park by float plane or boat, with the most popular region being Brooks Falls. Thousands of visitors from all over the world arrive at Brooks Falls each year to view brown bears feasting on salmon. The Brooks Falls Platform is the most popular location in Katmai for observing bears and salmon, where 10+ bears may be within eyesight at any given time. The platform holds up to 40 people, and busy days may call for 1-hour time limits to allow for fair viewing. Other popular activities in the park are fishing, hiking, backpacking, and boating.

We are hiking down the trail to Brooks Falls when we see an adolescent brown bear round the corner and come running toward us. Terrified, we swiftly move off the trail and let the bear pass. Seconds later, we see a large, likely dominant, male bear round the same corner, though luckily he moves off in another direction. I guess people weren't kidding when they said this place is teeming with bears, we nervously exclaim to one another. Onwards to the falls overlook we go. Waiting for us are numerous hungry bears feeding on a seemingly endless supply of salmon. At almost 10pm, we decide to head back to the campsite for some much-needed rest, hoping there aren't any surprise bear encounters on the trail this time around. We safely make it back to the tent, set our alarm, and are asleep within minutes... only to do it all again the next day.

LOCATION Alaska
PARK SIZE 4,093,077 acres
ICONIC FEATURE Brown bear viewing at Brooks Falls
BEST SEASON Summer
VISIT TIME Highlights of the Brooks Falls area in 1-2 days, though the park is best explored in 5-7 days.

STAY Brooks Falls Lodge or nearby Brooks Fall Campground
MUST HIKE Brooks Falls Trail, or explore Katmai's backcountry via unmaintained social trails.
PHOTO TIP When viewing bears at Brooks Falls, be sure to get out on the platforms as early as possible to beat the crowds and ensure softer light for your photos. Don't forget your telephoto lens!

35

KENAI FJORDS NATIONAL PARK

Epic Views On & Off Land

Kenai Fjords National Park is located in south-central Alaska, on the edge of the North Pacific Ocean, by the quaint town of Seward. The majority of Kenai Fjords is only accessible by boat, plane, or hiking, since very few roads exist in the park. One of the most popular sections of the park is the Exit Glacier area, where visitors can arrive by car or bus and have access to incredible hiking, backpacking, and camping. Another common activity is taking a tour-boat cruise to explore tidewater glaciers and marine wildlife. These often depart from Seward and some operators, such as Major Marine Tours, include commentary by knowledgeable park rangers.

LOCATION Alaska
PARK SIZE 603,130 acres
ICONIC FEATURE Harding Icefield
BEST SEASON Summer
VISIT TIME Highlights in 1-2 days, or best explored in 3-4 days
STAY Camp at Exit Glacier Campground, or stay in the town of Seward.
MUST HIKE Harding Icefield Trail, or nearby Glacier Overlook and Exit Glacier Overlook Trails
PHOTO TIP Take a ranger-narrated boat tour departing from Seward, which offers the chance to photograph marine life, seabirds, and magnificent tidewater glaciers.

"We reach the top and are blown away by the view, for before us lies a horizon of ice and snow that stretches as far as we can see."

We haul our backpacks up the steep Harding Icefield trail. With a gain in elevation of 1,000 ft / 305 m for every mile we hike, it quickly becomes apparent that the ranger wasn't fooling around when they said it was a strenuous trail. With epic views of Exit Glacier, lush cottonwood forests, and heather-filled meadows along the way… I guess it's not all bad. We reach the top and are blown away by the view, for before us lies a horizon of ice and snow that stretches as far as we can see. After our tent is set up for the night, we sit back and watch a golden sunset over the ice. The moon rises and creates a soft glow over the scene, and that's our cue to retreat into the warmth of our sleeping bags.

36

KINGS CANYON NATIONAL PARK

The Sierras' Secluded Gem

John Muir famously dubbed Kings Canyon "a rival to Yosemite" and even proclaimed it was a "grander valley of the same kind." We found the park to hold many similarities to Yosemite, but in contrast Kings Canyon felt surprisingly secluded and overall much more serene. The park is home to towering mountain peaks, lush meadows, powerful waterfalls, swift-flowing rivers, and some of the world's largest sequoia trees. There are opportunities for scenic driving, day hiking, camping, backpacking, rock climbing, fishing, and horseback riding.

LOCATION California
PARK SIZE 461,901 acres
ICONIC FEATURE Kings Canyon Scenic Byway
BEST SEASON Summer and fall
VISIT TIME Highlights in 1-2 days, or best explored alongside Sequoia National Park in 2-3 days

STAY Camp at the Cedar Grove Campground, or stay in comfort at John Muir Lodge.
MUST HIKE Zumwalt Meadows and Roaring Falls
PHOTO TIP Shoot golden afternoon light at Zumwalt Meadows, and consider a backcountry trek along Rae Lakes Loop for epic photo opportunities.

We don't know what to expect from Kings Canyon National Park. Driving the scenic byway into one of the deepest canyons in the country feels wild and almost otherworldly. We drive for hours without seeing more than a couple of cars and have every lookout and trail all to ourselves. It seems that all the tourists are busy exploring Yosemite and are clueless to the Sierras' secluded sister. As we stroll around Zumwalt Meadows, we are struck by the sheer beauty of the park's towering granite walls and overall peacefulness. It's almost as if Mother Nature knows what she has been hiding all along, and is quietly smiling at our wonder.

"If you want to see the glories of the Sierra canyons with minimal human disturbance, Kings Canyon ought to be your place. Some easy strolls will show what Yosemite was like in the 19th century." – *Bill Tweed*

37

KOBUK VALLEY NATIONAL PARK

Arctic Sand Dunes

Kobuk Valley is one of the most remote national parks in the country. Located in the Arctic Circle of northwest Alaska, the park is only accessible by plane or boat in summer, and by snowmobile, dogsled, or plane during winter. Despite its isolation, Kobuk Valley National Park boasts an array of outdoor activities, including flightseeing tours, backpacking, rafting, fishing, and hiking. It's also home to North America's largest Arctic dune field, the Great Kobuk Sand Dunes. Visitors can experience this unique location by wheeled aircraft that land directly on the sand, or by float plane on the Kobuk River (which requires trekking across tundra to the dunes).

Our plane soars above grassy tundra, Arctic sand dunes, and the mighty Kobuk River. Kevin, our pilot, dips to the left and points out a grizzly bear lumbering across the meadow below. We spot five more bears before landing the plane inside the park, confirming just how wild and untamed Kobuk Valley really is. We walk along the riverbank, spotting wolf prints and pushing our way through brush. A ranger back in Bettles told us that you could travel through the park for days without seeing another person, and that Kobuk Valley is more traveled by caribou than humans. What a privilege it is to experience a place that man is yet to control.

LOCATION Alaska
PARK SIZE 1,750,717 acres
ICONIC FEATURE Great Kobuk Sand Dunes
BEST SEASON Summer
VISIT TIME Flightseeing tour in 1 day, or a longer adventure over 5-7 days.
STAY Backcountry camp in the park, or stay in the nearby town of Bettles.
MUST HIKE There are no maintained trails in Kobuk Valley, but solo or guided backpacking and rafting adventures can be taken within the park.
PHOTO TIP Visiting during the park's annual caribou migration would be an incredible opportunity to take photographs.

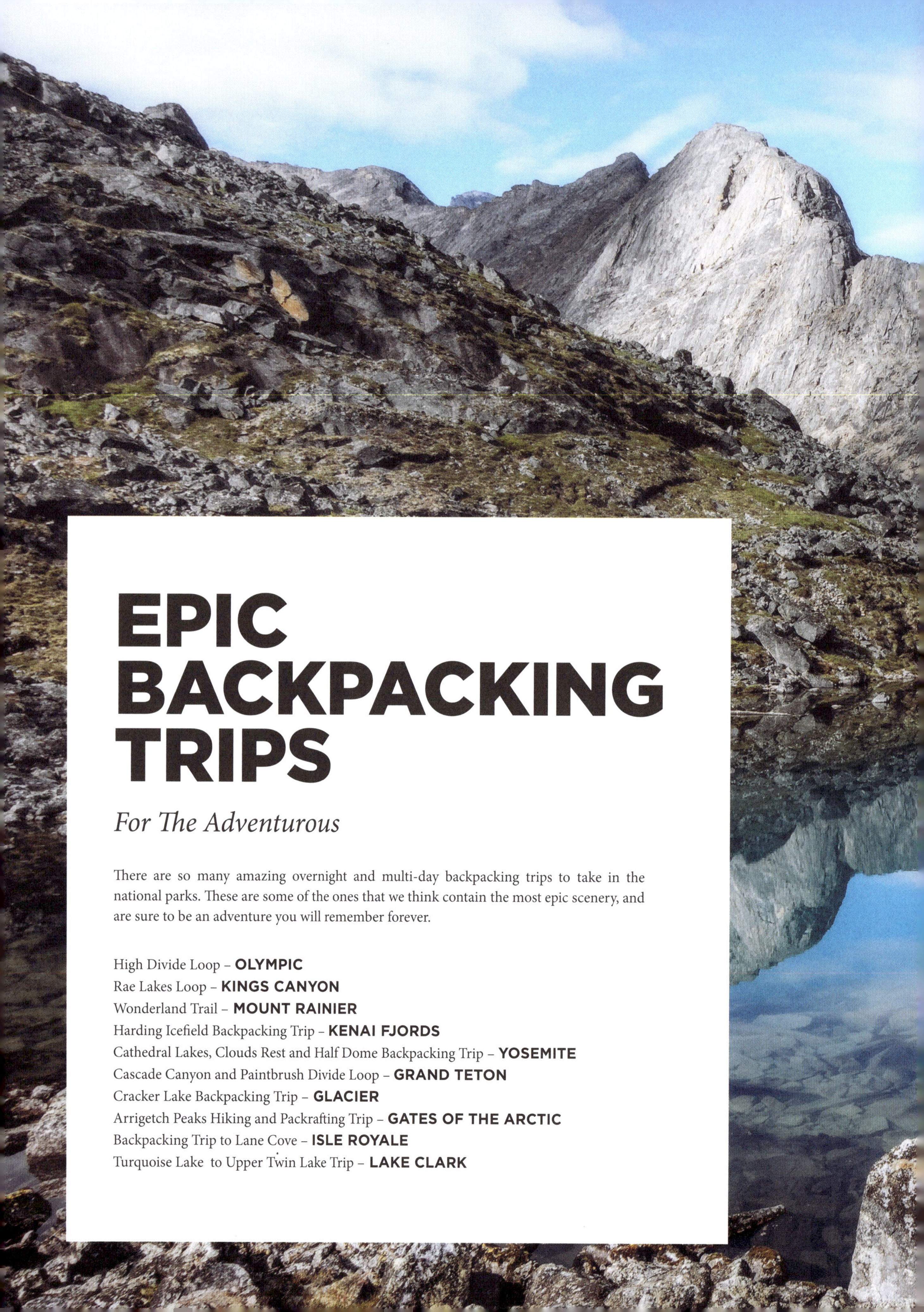

EPIC BACKPACKING TRIPS

For The Adventurous

There are so many amazing overnight and multi-day backpacking trips to take in the national parks. These are some of the ones that we think contain the most epic scenery, and are sure to be an adventure you will remember forever.

High Divide Loop – **OLYMPIC**
Rae Lakes Loop – **KINGS CANYON**
Wonderland Trail – **MOUNT RAINIER**
Harding Icefield Backpacking Trip – **KENAI FJORDS**
Cathedral Lakes, Clouds Rest and Half Dome Backpacking Trip – **YOSEMITE**
Cascade Canyon and Paintbrush Divide Loop – **GRAND TETON**
Cracker Lake Backpacking Trip – **GLACIER**
Arrigetch Peaks Hiking and Packrafting Trip – **GATES OF THE ARCTIC**
Backpacking Trip to Lane Cove – **ISLE ROYALE**
Turquoise Lake to Upper Twin Lake Trip – **LAKE CLARK**

38

LAKE CLARK NATIONAL PARK & PRESERVE

Turquoise Lakes & Blueberry Pancakes

There was tough competition, but Lake Clark National Park was probably our favorite of the entire trip. It earned this spot for its beauty, wildlife, history, and wonderful people. Lake Clark National Park is located 100 miles southwest of Anchorage and can only be accessed by plane. The park is home to some of Alaska's most breathtaking scenery: jagged mountain peaks, active volcanoes, impressive glaciers, lush vegetation, thundering waterfalls, the largest lake in the state, and a lively coastline. Visitors have a choice of various activities in the park, including flightseeing, hiking, fishing, kayaking, camping, berry picking, and relaxing by one of the many turquoise lakes. If you love nature, then you will fall head over heels for Lake Clark National Park.

LOCATION Alaska
PARK SIZE 4,030,015 acres
ICONIC FEATURE Twin Lakes and Dick Proenneke's cabin
BEST SEASON Summer
VISIT TIME Highlights of one area in 1-2 days, or best explored in 4-6 days

STAY Base yourself in Port Alsworth, backcountry camp in the park, or stay in a privately-owned wilderness cabin.
MUST HIKE Hope Creek Valley and Emerson Creek Falls, both unmaintained social trails leading from Upper Twin Lake
PHOTO TIP Consider visiting the Chinitna Bay region of the park to photograph coastal brown bears feasting on salmon – and don't forget your telephoto lens!

"Eight and a half miles can be covered in minutes in a car on an expressway, but what does a man see? What he gains in time he loses in benefit to his body and mind."

– Richard Proenneke

Many visitors come to Lake Clark to see Richard (Dick) Proenneke's cabin on Upper Twin Lake. At age 51, Dick decided that the typical 50-hour work week wasn't the life he was seeking, so he moved to Alaska "to do a thing to completion." He built a cabin on Upper Twin Lake with only hand tools he had made himself, and went on to live alone in the wilderness for more than 30 years. Dick kept journals of his time living in the park and exploring its wonders, which were later made into a book by Sam Keith: "One Man's Wilderness: An Alaskan Odyssey."

"Think of all the splendors that bespeak Alaska. Glaciers, volcanoes, alpine spires, wild rivers, lakes with grayling on the rise. Picture coasts feathered with countless seabirds. Imagine dense forests and farsweeping tundra, herds of caribou, great roving bears. Now concentrate all these and more into less than one percent of the state – and behold the Lake Clark region, Alaska's epitome."

– *John Kauffmann*

The sun is going down, and I'm swinging by the lake on a handmade wooden bench. We just experienced one of those days that feels too good to be true. It all started with a breakfast of pancakes made with wild blueberries we had picked on our hike yesterday. Afterwards, we paddled a canoe along the glassy waters of Upper Twin Lake, watching the mountains light up in the morning sun. Our afternoon was spent hiking up beautiful Emerson Creek to a hidden waterfall, followed by a refreshing dip in the lake. Dinner was freshly caught trout from just outside our cabin, shared with our host and paired with a side of a great conversation. We just spotted some bears on the mountainside across the lake and now I'm sitting here writing in my journal. Life really cannot get much better than this.

39

LASSEN VOLCANIC NATIONAL PARK

Endless Geothermal Wonders

Lassen Volcanic National Park's current geothermal activity and violent volcanic history make it a fascinating place to visit. Although it's still an active volcano, Lassen hasn't had a major eruption since 1915, when it spurted steam, ash, and gas some 30,000 ft / 9,000 m into the atmosphere. Visitors flock to the park in all seasons to discover colorful mountain vistas, forests of conifer trees, a wide range of wildlife, and countless geothermal hot spots. Another draw to visit the park is the journey along the highest road in the Cascade Mountains, since the main park road reaches 8,512 ft / 2,594 m as it travels by Lassen Peak.

LOCATION California
PARK SIZE 106,452 acres
ICONIC FEATURE Manzanita Lake
BEST SEASON Summer and fall
VISIT TIME Highlights in 1 day, or best explored in 2 days

STAY Manzanita Lake camping cabins or south of the park at St. Bernard Lodge
MUST HIKE Bumpass Hell and Cinder Cone trails
PHOTO TIP Hike up Cinder Cone at sunrise to capture lone trees on the Painted Dunes and 360-degree mountain views.

"A hot breakfast and shower can wait; views like these are worth being a little uncomfortable for."

It's 5 a.m. as we crawl out of the van, grab a quick snack, and head for the Cinder Cone Trail. We stumble along in the pre-sunrise darkness, illuminating the steps before us with headlamps. Scrambling up some 846 ft / 257 m of loose rock at high altitude is a physical and mental challenge. Freezing cold wind threatens to topple us over the second we reach the summit, but not even that can put a damper on the incredible 360-degree mountain views. We stay and watch the sunrise and huddle together to keep warm. A hot breakfast and shower can wait; views like these are worth being a little uncomfortable for.

40

MAMMOTH CAVE NATIONAL PARK

Journey To The Center Of Kentucky

Mammoth Cave National Park is home to the world's longest recorded cave system. Estimated to have begun forming around 10 million years ago, explorers have mapped more than 405 mi / 652 km of cave passages. Most visitors arrive at the park to explore the labyrinth of subterranean caverns, and various ranger-led cave tours are offered. The most well-known section of Mammoth Cave is arguably the Frozen Niagara, a cave rock formation that appears as if an underground waterfall has been frozen in time. The park also has many wonders above ground, including picturesque hiking trails and the Green River's interesting cultural history.

LOCATION Kentucky
PARK SIZE 52,830 acres
ICONIC FEATURE Mammoth Cave itself
BEST SEASON Year round, though less crowded in early spring, fall, and winter
VISIT TIME Best explored in 1-2 days
STAY The Lodge at Mammoth Cave or Mammoth Cave Campground
MUST HIKE Grand Avenue Cave tour and the River Styx Spring Trail
PHOTO TIP Consider capturing images above ground, such as along trails surrounding the Green River. Soft afternoon light provides a fairy-tale scene and ample photo opportunities.

Our morning has been spent touring the Grand Avenue of Mammoth Cave. It had been an incredible experience, but now we craved above-ground beauty like sunshine, grass, and lush trees. We set off hiking, but within minutes the heavens opened and began dumping rain. We huddled under a small shelter and hoped the lightning wasn't heading our way. Luckily, the storm blew over as quickly as it had arrived, leaving a fairy-tale scene in its path. Low fog had formed along the Green River, and leaves sparkled as sunrays peeked through the clouds. It was the perfect example of how the main attraction of a park isn't necessarily the only thing worth seeing.

"A grand, gloomy and peculiar place."

– *Stephen Bishop*

41

MESA VERDE NATIONAL PARK

An Archeological Wonder

Mesa Verde National Park was created to safeguard the history of the Ancestral Puebloan people, who are said to have lived there from 550-1300 A.D. The park is home to nearly 5,000 archeological sites and 600 cliff dwellings, nestled 2,000 feet above the Montezuma Valley. Ranger-led tours are offered for visitors to explore the elaborate cliff dwellings, with some being somewhat strenuous and others more easily accessible. Many of Mesa Verde's cliff dwellings can be viewed from park roads and overlooks, such as Sun Point Overlook which offers a glimpse of Cliff Palace.

LOCATION Colorado

PARK SIZE 52,485 acres

ICONIC FEATURE Cliff Palace and Balcony House

BEST SEASON Late spring and summer for the largest choice of ranger-led tours

VISIT TIME Best explored in 1-2 days

STAY Camp at Morefield Campground, or stay in comfort at Far View Lodge.

MUST HIKE Take a tour of the cliff dwellings at Cliff Palace or Balcony House, or hike the Petroglyph Point Trail.

PHOTO TIP The park runs a handful of sunrise cliff dwelling tours each year, which would be ideal for capturing golden light on the structures around surrounding cliffs.

"We enter Balcony House and are greeted by an incredible display of primitive rooms, intricate kivas, and a glimpse into the life of living cliffside."

Our guide is sharing stories of the ancient Puebloan people as we make our way toward Balcony House, one of the many cliff dwellings at Mesa Verde. We arrive at the base of a 33 ft / 10 m high ladder, and he tells us there's no turning around once you enter the site. We enter Balcony House and are greeted by an incredible display of primitive rooms, intricate kivas, and a glimpse into the life of living cliffside. We feel incredibly privileged to have witnessed such a preserved wonder and hope many more people get the chance in the years to come.

MOUNT RAINIER NATIONAL PARK

A Wonderland Of Beauty & Grandeur

Mount Rainier National Park is one of those special places that captivates anyone who experiences it. Home to breathtaking mountain vistas, lush hiking trails, campsites among pine trees, and wildflower-clad meadows, visitors are treated to limitless opportunities for adventure. The park has five major areas to explore, all forming a circle around Mount Rainier: Paradise, Sunrise, Longmire, Ohanapecosh, and Carbon/Mowich. Paradise is the most popular section to explore due to its easy accessibility from Seattle, iconic hiking trails, abundant wildflowers, and convenient infrastructure.

LOCATION Washington

PARK SIZE 236,381 acres

ICONIC FEATURE Mount Rainier (14,410 ft / 4,392 m)

BEST SEASON Summer and early fall

VISIT TIME Highlights in 1-2 days, or best explored in 3-4 days

STAY Camp at one of the park-run campgrounds, or stay in comfort at the historic Paradise Inn.

MUST HIKE Skyline Trail Loop, Mt. Fremont Lookout Trail, and Tolmie Peak Trail

PHOTO TIP Wildflower season is the best time to capture photos in the park. This typically falls between mid-July to mid-August, but varies each year depending on conditions.

"... the most luxuriant and the most extravagantly beautiful of all the alpine gardens I have ever beheld in all my mountain-top wanderings."

– John Muir

We spend our days in the park rising to capture sunrise, returning to the van during the busy hours, and hitting the trails again during late afternoon hours. The view of Mount Rainier towering above us never becomes unremarkable, leaving us in awe each time we round a bend in the trail and witness a different perspective. We hike through meadows filled with wildflowers, through forests of thick pines, and by the refreshing spray of waterfalls. It's a busy park, yet we continually find ourselves on lesser-known trails, soaking in the magnificent views to the sounds of foraging squirrels and distant rocks falling.

LEAST CROWDED PARKS

For Those Seeking Solitude

America's national parks are getting busier each year, and it can be challenging at times to escape the crowds. We typically found ourselves enjoying the more secluded and less crowded national parks during our visit to all 59.

To clarify, this isn't just another list of statistics of the least-visited national parks; instead, this is a first-hand report of which parks were actually the least crowded during our 2017 road trip. We found that least crowded and least visited didn't always mean the same thing, as some national parks are tiny and felt very busy despite having small visitor numbers.

THEODORE ROOSEVELT
BLACK CANYON OF THE GUNNISON
AMERICAN SAMOA
GUADALUPE MOUNTAINS
BIG BEND
GREAT BASIN
GREAT SAND DUNES
LAKE CLARK
GATES OF THE ARCTIC
VOYAGEURS
NORTH CASCADES
KINGS CANYON
LASSEN VOLCANIC
MAMMOTH CAVE
KOBUK VALLEY

American Samoa

43

NORTH CASCADES NATIONAL PARK

The American Alps

North Cascades National Park is home to breathtaking mountain peaks, hundreds of glaciers, forested valleys, vibrant lakes, and endless opportunities for adventure. Consisting of two main units, the North and South sections, the park also offers two adjoining recreation areas for visitors to explore: Ross Lakes and Lake Chelan. These three areas make up the North Cascades National Park Service Complex, the only one of its kind in the country. The park has numerous accessible trails and overlooks, though it's best explored by getting off the main highway and out into the backcountry.

LOCATION Washington
PARK SIZE 684,000 acres
ICONIC FEATURE North Cascade Highway and various scenic overlooks and trails
BEST SEASON Summer and early fall
VISIT TIME Highlights in 1-2 days, or best explored in 3-4 days
STAY Camp at one of many campgrounds in the park or in nearby towns such as Marblemont and Winthrop.
MUST HIKE Cascade Pass, Trappers Peak, and Blue Lake trails
PHOTO TIP Get out into the backcountry for epic photography opportunities, such as Mount Shuksan at sunrise and Trappers Peak at sunset.

We have climbed almost 3,000 ft / 914 m in elevation and my lungs are making their presence known. It's time for a quick rest before pushing to the summit of Trapper Peak. We sit down next to the trail and enjoy some wild blueberries as our friends give their infant daughter a bottle. I love that about the national parks, how they are for all of us to enjoy, young, old, families, singles… We are so fortunate to have these protected wild places. Onwards we climb to the summit, arriving shortly before sunset. The sky turns shades of pink and yellow, casting a glow on the jagged peaks around us. It is quite the sight to behold.

"I went out in my alpine yard and there it was... hundreds of miles of pure snow-covered rocks and virgin lakes and high timber... Below, instead of the world, I saw a sea of marshmallow clouds."

– Jack Kerouac

44

OLYMPIC NATIONAL PARK

Nature's Finest Diversity

Olympic National Park has it all: beautiful coastline, lush rain forests, and soaring mountains. Located in the northwestern corner of Washington State, the Olympic Peninsula is a three-hour drive from Seattle, and can also be accessed by ferry from Canada. The park is full of natural beauty, diversity, and endless things to do – making it one of the most visited parks in the country. Popular visitor activities include hiking, camping, tide-pooling, boating, fishing, wildlife viewing, and photography.

LOCATION Washington

PARK SIZE 922,651 acres

ICONIC FEATURE Hoh Rain Forest

BEST SEASON Spring through fall

VISIT TIME Highlights in 1-2 days, or best explored in 3-4 days

STAY Olympic has numerous park-run campgrounds, or there is the option to stay at one of the park's lodges, such as the Kalaloch Lodge.

MUST HIKE Hall of Mosses, Marymere Falls, and Mount Storm King trails. Strolling along Ruby Beach is another a must-do.

PHOTO TIP The Hoh Rain Forest, Sul Doc Falls, and Ruby Beach make for scenic photography spots.

We begin down the Hall of Mosses trail and within seconds are surrounded by towering evergreen giants and moss-laden maples. Everything is lush and vibrant green in this magnificent rainforest, and each turn brings another canopy of surprises. The forest floor is thickly blanketed with moss and ferns. The best way to describe it would be enchanting… This trail is beyond enchanting. We stroll for hours along the trail, despite being less than a mile, for we are determined to take in every corner of this magical place.

"We stroll for hours along the trail, despite being less than a mile, for we are determined to take in every corner of this magical place."

45

PETRIFIED FOREST NATIONAL PARK

Prehistoric Playground

Often overshadowed by Arizona's grander parks, Petrified Forest is bursting with natural beauty and prehistoric remains. The park is home to the world's largest collection of petrified wood, which is said to have begun its life cycle some 225 million years ago. In addition, Petrified Forest boasts dinosaur fossils, colorful badlands, picturesque hiking trails, petroglyphs, and ancient ruins from primitive cultures. History junkies can also explore the section of the famous Route 66, that intersects the park, offering a glimpse into the mid-20th century golden age of travel.

LOCATION Arizona
PARK SIZE 221,390 acres
ICONIC FEATURE Petrified wood and dinosaur fossils
BEST SEASON Year round
VISIT TIME Best explored in 1-2 days
STAY Backcountry camp in the park, or stay in the nearby town of Holbrook.
MUST HIKE Crystal Forest Trail and Giant Logs Trail
PHOTO TIP Capture golden afternoon light at Crystal Forest, and photograph sunset from various lookouts along the Blue Mesa Loop.

"Each turn features another incredibly preserved slice of petrified wood, leaving us in complete awe of nature's beauty and force."

We are usually fairly brisk hikers, yet we find ourselves spending hours wandering around Crystal Forest's short 0.75 mi / 1.2 km loop. Each turn features another incredibly preserved slice of petrified wood, leaving us in complete awe of nature's beauty and force. We stop at each informational sign and slowly begin to fathom how the colorful wood was created over the past millions of years. The golden afternoon sun brings out rich hues in the landscape, and we can't help but fill our camera's memory cards with countless photos. We leave the park that night with a strong sense of gratitude for this wonderful earth we call home.

46

PINNACLES NATIONAL PARK

Caves, Condors & Cliffs

Pinnacles is one of the United States' youngest national parks, only established in 2013 by the Obama administration. The park is split into two districts, the west side being known for its talus caves, and the east side boasting an established campground and the main park visitor center. Both districts have ample opportunities to go hiking, caving, bird-watching, climbing, and more. The Pinnacles themselves refer to a concentrated region of colorful rocks, elaborate cliffs, and talus caves. They were said to have been formed by volcanic activity some 23 million years ago and have eroded since then into what visitors witness throughout the park today.

LOCATION California
PARK SIZE 26,000 acres
ICONIC FEATURE The Pinnacles geologic formations
BEST SEASON Year round, though busiest during summer
VISIT TIME Best explored in 1-2 days
STAY Camp at the Pinnacles Campground on the east side of the park.

MUST HIKE Moses Spring Trail and High Peaks Trail to Bear Gulch Loop
PHOTO TIP High Peaks Overlook is a beautiful spot for sunset photography. Many bird photographers also come to Pinnacles to capture images of the unique California Condor.

I've lost sight of Matthew in the dark cave and call out for him to slow down. We forgot our headlamps and are relying on our phones to illuminate the path. Around each corner, we seem to come across yet another talus cave, tunnel, or moss-covered rock formation. Water is running though this particular cave and the only voices we hear are our own echoes. It's a humbling feeling walking through caves this ancient, never knowing what we will find around the next bend, and wondering at what point the trail will start looping back around.

"It's a humbling feeling walking through caves this ancient, never knowing what we will find around the next bend."

WELCOME
TO
PINNACLES
NATIONAL
PARK
NATIONAL
PARK
SERVICE

47

REDWOOD NATIONAL & STATE PARK

Walk Among Giants

Redwood National Park also encompasses three local state parks: Jedediah Smith Redwoods, Del Norte Coast, and Prairie Creek State Parks. Not surprisingly, these parks are most famous for their ancient redwood trees, which may well be the tallest trees (and tallest living things) on the planet. Visitors are attracted to the parks for forest trekking, coastal walking, photography, backpacking, wildlife viewing, tide-pooling, biking, kayaking, and scenic driving.

LOCATION California

PARK SIZE 131,983 acres

ICONIC FEATURE Ancient redwood trees averaging 500-700 years in age

BEST SEASON Year round, though most lush in Spring

VISIT TIME Highlights in 1 day, or best explored in 2-3 days

STAY Towns like Crescent City and Trinidad have numerous lodging options and are located near park attractions.

MUST HIKE Boy Scout Tree Trail in Jedediah Smith Redwoods State Park

PHOTO TIP Capture beautiful redwoods and lush ferns along the Prairie Creek Trail, Boy Scout Trail, and Tall Trees Grove Trail.

"The redwoods, once seen, leave a mark or create a vision that stays with you always. The feeling they produce is not transferable. From them comes silence and awe. It's not only their unbelievable stature, nor the color which seems to shift and vary under your eyes, no, they are not like any trees we know, they are ambassadors from another time." – *John Steinbeck*

It is surreal and humbling walking among the giant redwoods. Their canopy soars some 300 ft / 91 m above us and many of their trunks are a magnificent 16-20 ft / 4-6 m in diameter. How many people have these ancient trees observed walking by them? What stories do they hold? How many times have they been threatened by deforestation? Probably more times than we could imagine, making us deeply thankful for their modern-day protection and our privilege of experiencing their beauty.

48

ROCKY MOUNTAIN NATIONAL PARK

High On Adventure

Rocky Mountain National Park is home to one of Colorado's most diverse and magnificent wilderness areas. Best known for its impressive mountain peaks, Rocky Mountain National Park is teeming with alpine lakes, lush meadows, unique wildlife, and endless miles of hiking trails. The park is split into two main sections, east and west of the Continental Divide, with the famed Trail Ridge Road connecting the two. The east side of the park receives more visitors due to its accessibility from Denver, proximity to the quaint town of Estes Park, and various opportunities for adventure.

LOCATION Colorado
PARK SIZE 265,795 acres
ICONIC FEATURE Trail Ridge Road, and Dream Lake
BEST SEASON Summer
VISIT TIME Highlights in 1-2 days, or best explored in 3-4 days
STAY Camp at Moraine Park Campground, or stay in nearby Estes Park.

MUST HIKE Emerald Lake Trail, Sprague Lake Trail, and Sky Pond Lake Trail
PHOTO TIP Capture sunrise at Dream Lake, which is magnificent during any season. Driving the Trail Ridge Road during summer is a great way to capture images of the park's mountain peaks and wildlife such as elk.

Despite having lived in nearby Boulder for almost two years, we are bursting with excitement to be back at Rocky Mountain. It's impossible to tire of this park's epic views, even after spending countless days exploring the many backcountry hikes, alpine lakes, and pine forests. Rocky Mountain is where it all started for us... It was our first local park when we relocated to America, and where our love for the outdoors was truly ingrained. Being back on our favorite trails feels nostalgic and we make an effort to soak in every moment.

"Rocky Mountain is where it all started for us... It was our first local park when we relocated to America, and where our love for the outdoors was truly ingrained."

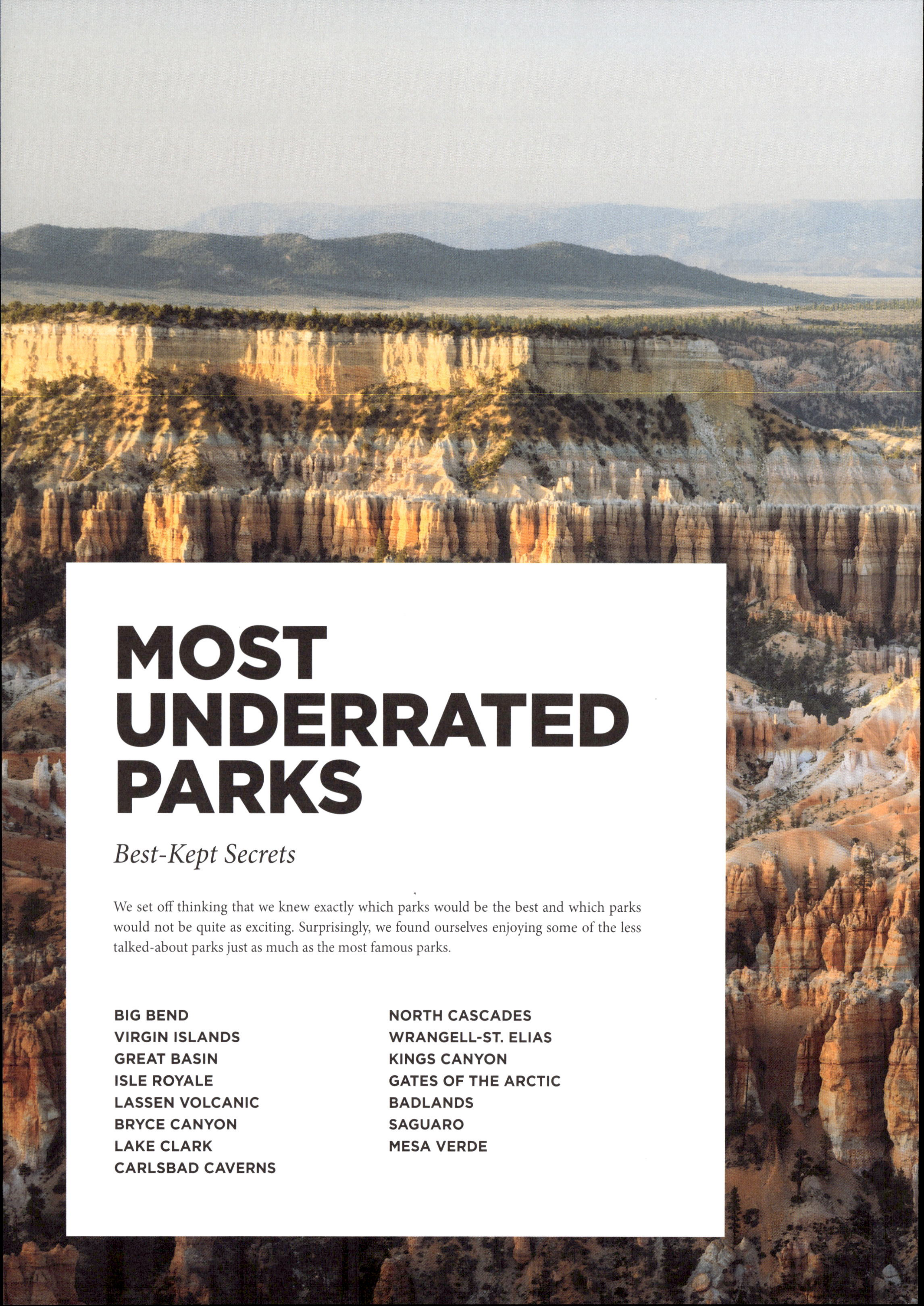

MOST UNDERRATED PARKS

Best-Kept Secrets

We set off thinking that we knew exactly which parks would be the best and which parks would not be quite as exciting. Surprisingly, we found ourselves enjoying some of the less talked-about parks just as much as the most famous parks.

BIG BEND
VIRGIN ISLANDS
GREAT BASIN
ISLE ROYALE
LASSEN VOLCANIC
BRYCE CANYON
LAKE CLARK
CARLSBAD CAVERNS
NORTH CASCADES
WRANGELL-ST. ELIAS
KINGS CANYON
GATES OF THE ARCTIC
BADLANDS
SAGUARO
MESA VERDE

Bryce Canyon

SAGUARO NATIONAL PARK

Icon of the Southwest

Saguaro is a lesser-known national park, likely because it's simply not as dramatic or as romanticized as places like Yosemite and Zion. In contrast, Saguaro National Park is less crowded, has fewer trails, and less infrastructure. Don't let that fool you though, as the park is home to unique natural sights, peaceful scenes, and an icon of the Southwest: the impressive saguaro cactus. The park's main purpose is to protect healthy forests of saguaro cacti within the Sonoran Desert. Split into two sections east and west of Tucson, each park district provides beautiful scenery, scenic drives, and interesting hiking trails.

LOCATION Arizona
PARK SIZE 91,716 acres
ICONIC FEATURE The Saguaro cactus
BEST SEASON Fall through spring
VISIT TIME Best explored in 1-2 days

STAY Nearby Tucson has a range of accommodation options.
MUST HIKE Cactus Forest Trail and King Canyon Trail
PHOTO TIP The golden hour before sunset is best captured along Cactus Forest Loop Drive in the Rincon Mountain District.

Our van has been in the shop all day and we are eager to get back out exploring. As sunset nears, we finally get moving and head straight toward the national park. We make our way to the beginning of Cactus Forest Loop Drive in hopes of capturing the park's most iconic beauty, the saguaro cactus. Golden light has blanketed the desert landscape with rich hues of yellow and orange, enhancing the tall saguaro trees scattered around us. It's a magical scene and we hardly come across another soul. This peacefulness is becoming a common theme of our parks adventure, where everyone seems to leave just when the light gets golden and wildlife begin making their appearances.

"Golden light has blanketed the desert landscape with rich hues of yellow and orange, enhancing the tall saguaro trees scattered around us."

50

SEQUOIA NATIONAL PARK

The Land Of Giants

Visitors come from all over the world to Sequoia National Park with the aim of seeing the world's largest trees. As we saw in other parks around California and Nevada, nearby coastal redwoods are the tallest trees in the world, and bristlecone pines are the oldest trees, but sequoias take the lead for the largest trees in the world by cubic volume. The largest of all is said to be the General Sherman, with an estimated age of between 2,300 and 2,700 years old and a whopping 36.5 ft / 11.1 m in trunk diameter. Other popular sights in the park include Big Trees Trail, Moro Rock, Tunnel Log, and summiting Mount Whitney (the tallest mountain in the lower 48 U.S. states, at 14,505 ft / 4,421 m).

It's challenging to describe the exact feeling of standing next to the world's largest tree. Impossible to view in entirety at one glance or from a single angle, the General Sherman really is a natural giant. Similar to a city skyscraper, standing alongside a sequoia tree instantly makes you feel small and insignificant in the best way possible. As we amble through the forest, we stare in wonder at each tree's almost inconceivable mass, wondering what secrets these gentle giants must hold. We are humbled standing in their presence, an experience that every person on this planet could benefit from.

LOCATION California
PARK SIZE 404,063 acres
ICONIC FEATURE The General Sherman tree
BEST SEASON Summer and fall
VISIT TIME Highlights in 1 day, or best explored alongside Kings Canyon National Park in 2-3 days

STAY Camp at centrally located Lodgepole Campground, or stay in comfort at Wuksachui Lodge.
MUST HIKE Big Trees Trail
PHOTO TIP The iconic 'Tunnel Log' makes for a fun photo opportunity, and of course photographing the world-famous General Sherman tree is a must.

"As we amble through the forest, we stare in wonder at each tree's almost inconceivable mass, wondering what secrets these gentle giants must hold."

51

SHENANDOAH NATIONAL PARK

An Escape Into Nature

Nestled in the lush Blue Ridge Mountains, Shenandoah National Park feels like a world away from the hustle and bustle of the cities surrounding it. Visitors come from near and far to tour the famed Skyline Drive, and to go hiking, camping, fishing, bicycling, rock climbing, and horseback riding. The park is long and narrow, with 75 scenic lookouts dotted along the 105 mi / 169 km of Skyline Drive, including numerous trails to rocky overlooks, thick forests, and cascading waterfalls. Whether visited in only a few hours or explored for a week, Shenandoah National Park has something for everyone to enjoy.

LOCATION Virginia
PARK SIZE 197,438 acres
ICONIC FEATURE Skyline Drive
BEST SEASON Year round
VISIT TIME Highlights in 1 day, or best explored in 2-3 days

STAY Camp at Big Meadows Campground, or stay at Big Meadows Lodge.
MUST HIKE Little Stony Man Cliffs and Old Rag Mountain Loop
PHOTO TIP Visit during the fall for colorful foliage along Skyline Drive and nearby Blue Ridge Parkway.

We arrive at the parking lot in the early morning, and it quickly becomes apparent that we aren't the only ones planning to hike Old Rag Mountain today. Off we set with enough water, snacks, and sunscreen to last us 9 mi / 14.5 km of relatively strenuous terrain. The trail climbs steeply through a lush forest, switchbacking its way up to the summit. We emerge from the trees to find our next challenge of boulder climbing and rock walking to the final lookout. Finally we reach the top of Old Rag, snap some photos, and find a quiet spot to eat lunch while taking in the spectacular view… Definitely worth braving the crowds for.

"If you drive to, say, Shenandoah National Park, of the Great Smoky Mountains, you'll get some appreciation for the scale and beauty of the outdoors. When you walk into it, then you see it in a completely different way. You discover it in a much slower, more majestic sort of way."

– Bill Bryson

52

THEODORE ROOSEVELT NATIONAL PARK

A Desolate Sanctuary

Theodore Roosevelt National Park is remote, wild, and filled with wonders. The park's three distinct units are home to diverse wildlife, rugged badlands, thriving grasslands, and pockets of solitude. The South and North Units are the largest and have the most options for exploring, while Elkhorn Ranch is the smallest unit, located midway between the two others. The park is also famous for being where President Theodore Roosevelt's love of nature began. After spending time ranching in the area, he would later go on to establish the US Forest Service, 18 national monuments, 5 national parks, 150 national forests, and numerous federal reserves – with a total of over 230 million acres of protected land.

LOCATION North Dakota
PARK SIZE 70,446 acres
ICONIC FEATURE Painted Canyon Overlook
BEST SEASON Spring and fall
VISIT TIME Best explored in 1-2 days
STAY Camp inside the park at Juniper or Cottonwood Campground, or stay in nearby towns such as Medora.
MUST HIKE Painted Canyon Nature Trail
PHOTO TIP Capture sunrise from Oxbow and Riverbend Overlooks and sunset from Painted Canyon Overlook.

Wild horses graze as families of prairie dogs scurry nearby. Bison stroll leisurely across the road, never batting an eyelid at us. White-tailed deer and pronghorn also roam the lands. We watch the sunset from Painted Canyon Overlook and share stories of adventure with newly-met, like-minded travelers. This place is wildly beautiful, and it surprises us how little we had heard of the park prior to our road trip. On our way out the next morning, we are greeted to a fiery sunrise over the plains, as if to remind us not to forget our time at the park and to be sure to visit again.

"Nothing could be more lonely and nothing more beautiful than the view at nightfall across the prairies to these huge hill masses, when the lengthening shadows had at last merged into one and the faint after-glow of the red sunset filled the west."

– Theodore Roosevelt

GOWESTY

53

VIRGIN ISLANDS NATIONAL PARK

An Escape Into Nature

Virgin Islands National Park is a tropical gem found tucked away in the Caribbean on the island of St. John. Although best known for its beautiful beaches, marine life, and snorkeling, the park is also brimming with ancient history, a vibrant culture, and numerous hiking trails. Human life on St. John dates back to between 1000 BC and 200 BC, with Spanish settlement thought to have started in the 1500s, followed by the Danish in the 1600s. As a result, the island is scattered with historic ruins for visitors to explore during their stay.

LOCATION United States Virgin Islands (USVI)

PARK SIZE 15,135 acres

ICONIC FEATURE Trunk Bay for its turquoise water and snorkeling

BEST SEASON Year round, though January-April generally see less rainfall and mosquitos

VISIT TIME Best explored in 3-5 days

STAY Cruz Bay has a range of accommodation options near the park.

MUST HIKE The Trunk Bay Underwater Trail is the USVI's unique snorkeling alternative.

PHOTO TIP Capture sunrise and sunset along one of the park's beautiful beaches, such as Trunk Bay, Maho Bay, Cinnamon Bay, and Hawksnest Bay.

We wake to the sun peeking through our tent and the sound of nature beginning its day. Like the nights prior, it had been a restless sleep outdoors due to the sticky humidity that is common in May. Again, like each day before, we throw on our swimsuits, run along the white sand some 30 steps to the water, dive straight in, and proceed to soak in the soft morning glow and solitude. It's hard to describe just how magical the crystal-clear turquoise water of St. John is. Everything about this island is enchanting, and we knew the second we arrived that we would return time and time again.

"Everything about this island is enchanting, and we knew the second we arrived that we would return time and time again."

54

VOYAGEURS NATIONAL PARK

Water-Based Wilderness

Voyageurs is a water-based park on the border between Minnesota, USA and Ontario, Canada. The park is best experienced by watercraft and is made up of four main lakes: Rainy, Kabetogama, Namakan, and Sand Point. Voyageurs is one of the only places in North America where visitors can witness and touch rocks half the age of Earth. These prehistoric rocks can be experienced by getting out on the water and exploring the park's many islands and sights, such as Ellsworth Rock Gardens. Other popular park activities include camping, fishing, hiking, swimming, and canoeing.

We arrive at Voyageurs just one day before they officially begin the summer season and boat tours. Instead, we find a local guide, Bill, who offers to take us out on the water. Bill tours us around the park, showing us all the best spots and sharing his years of local knowledge. He grew up exploring these same lakes and gives us some insight on how the park has changed over the years. He brings along his adorable dog, Riley, who sits at the front of the boat as if he is captain for the day. After a big day of exploring, we begin heading back to the mainland, and spot at least ten bald eagles along the way.

LOCATION Minnesota
PARK SIZE 218,054 acres
ICONIC FEATURE Ancient rocks and unique wildlife
BEST SEASON Spring through fall
VISIT TIME Best explored in 1-2 days
STAY Backcountry camp on one of the park's rocky islands, stay at Kettle Falls Historic Lodge, or base yourself out of Ash River or Woodenfrog Campground.

MUST HIKE Blind Ash Bay and Cruiser Lake trails
PHOTO TIP Voyageurs is a birders dream! Get out on the water with your zoom lens and capture wild bald eagles and other birds of prey.

Grand Teton

MOST SCENIC PARKS

A Feast For The Eyes

We kept a rating scale throughout our national parks journey, ranking each park for its scenery, trails, facilities, crowds, and how photogenic it was. These are the parks that ranked the highest for scenery, which took into account the landscapes and wildlife. We found these parks typically ranked the highest for hiking trails, and they were often also the most photogenic.

GRAND TETON
KENAI FJORDS
WRANGELL-ST. ELIAS
DENALI
MOUNT RAINIER
YOSEMITE
GLACIER BAY
LAKE CLARK
GLACIER
KATMAI
GATES OF THE ARCTIC
YELLOWSTONE
ZION
OLYMPIC
ROCKY MOUNTAIN

55

WIND CAVE NATIONAL PARK

A Hidden Gem Of The Dakotas

Wind Cave National Park is home to one of the world's most intricate cave networks and one of the last remaining mixed-grass prairies in the United States. There's ample to do in this small park, both underground and above the surface. The majority of visitors come to explore the park's cave system and there are numerous ranger-guided tours to choose from. Wind Cave is most famous for its boxwork cave formations and holds 95% of all boxwork calcite in the world. Above ground, visitors are welcomed by lush grasslands, an abundance of wildlife, and scenic trails.

LOCATION South Dakota

PARK SIZE 33,851 acres

ICONIC FEATURE Wind Cave and its unique boxwork cave formations

BEST SEASON Spring and summer

VISIT TIME Best explored in 1-2 days

STAY Camp at Elk Mountain Campground, or stay in the nearby towns of Hot Springs and Custer.

MUST HIKE Garden of Eden cave tour and Lookout Point Trail

PHOTO TIP It's challenging to capture images within the cave itself, since visitors are not allowed to use tripods or flash photography. We found the best photo opportunities were above ground, capturing wildlife roaming through the park.

"They say only five percent of the cave has been discovered. As we stroll past seemingly endless formations, it's almost impossible to imagine what the entire cave system might look like."

They say only five percent of the cave has been discovered. As we stroll past seemingly endless formations, it's almost impossible to imagine what the entire cave system might look like. The tour soon comes to an end and we emerge back into daylight, quickly jumping into the van to explore more of the park. Not too long after, we come across herds of bison roaming the plains and prairie dogs scuttling around. It's as though they have always called these grasslands home. A storm rolls in and we witness a dramatic sunset, the kind that is fiery red and warning us of impending rain. We head back to the campsite and settle in for a stormy night.

56

WRANGELL-ST. ELIAS NATIONAL PARK

America's Largest National Park

Wrangell-St. Elias National Park is a wild and isolated place. It's the largest national park in the country and – combined with neighboring parks – represents the world's largest international protected wilderness. Wrangell-St. Elias ranges in elevation from sea level to above 18,000 ft / 5,500 m, with snow-capped mountain peaks looming in every direction. There is nothing small about this magnificent park, and its beauty will imprint on any person that steps within its boundaries. Wrangell-St. Elias is also known for its copper-mining history, once the world's largest of its kind. Although the mines are now closed, visitors can tour the Kennecott Copper Mine and learn about the area's cultural history.

LOCATION Alaska
PARK SIZE 13,175,799 acres
ICONIC FEATURE Old mining town of Kennecott and nearby Root Glacier
BEST SEASON Summer
VISIT TIME Highlights in 2-3 days, or best explored on a week-long backcountry adventure
STAY Base yourself out of the historic Kennicott Glacier Lodge, or take a backcountry camping adventure.
MUST HIKE Root Glacier/Erie Mine Trail, or consider taking a guided ice-climbing tour on the glacier.
PHOTO TIP A flightseeing tour is the best way to capture the size and scale of Wrangell-St. Elias. Opt for an early morning or afternoon flight for optimal light conditions.

We soar above seemingly endless glaciers, intertwined rivers, and snow-capped mountain peaks on our way toward McCarthy, our gateway to Wrangell-St. Elias National Park. We land, take the bus to Kennicott Glacier Lodge, change into our hiking clothes, and set off to explore the park. The trail signs leading to Root Glacier inform us of bear activity in the area, and we spot some fresh scat along the way. We eventually reach the glacier and begin our search for vibrant pools and patterns in the ice. Careful not to trek near any crevasses, we hike until eventually finding the bluest glacier pool either of us have ever seen. What an incredible sight to behold!

"We soar above seemingly endless glaciers, intertwined rivers, and snow-capped mountain peaks..."

57

YELLOWSTONE NATIONAL PARK

The World's First National Park

Yellowstone is a world-renowned park, celebrated for its scenic views, abundant wildlife, hydrothermal features, and endless opportunities for adventure. The park has five main sections to explore: Old Faithful, Mammoth Hot Springs, Yellowstone Lake, Grand Canyon of the Yellowstone, and the Lamar Valley. It's no secret that Yellowstone sits on top of a supervolcano, said to be capable of erupting more than 240 cubic miles of magma. The park's many hydrothermal features are popular attractions for its 4,500,000+ million visitors each year, who come to witness one of the world's most impressive natural wonders.

LOCATION Wyoming, Montana, and Idaho
PARK SIZE 2,221,766 acres
ICONIC FEATURE Old Faithful Geyser
BEST SEASON Spring and fall
VISIT TIME Highlights in 1-2 days, or best explored in 3-5 days
STAY Camp at one of the park's many established campgrounds, or stay at a historic lodge, such as the Old Faithful Inn.

MUST HIKE Grand Prismatic Overlook, Mount Washburn, and Upper Geyser Basin trails
PHOTO TIP The Lamar Valley is the best location for photographing wildlife. Visit during sunrise and sunset for your best chance of seeing bears, wolves, and bison, and be sure to bring along a zoom lens.

Yellowstone was one of the first national parks we visited when beginning our travels in America. We are excited to be back with fresh eyes and a few more years of photography experience under our belts. We cruise into the parking lot of Old Faithful Inn, cook an early dinner, and head out on the Upper Geyser Basin Trail. Every corner brings another vibrant geothermal pool, bubbling mud pit, or steaming geyser. We encounter a few bison along the way, making sure to give them ample space as we pass by. Sunset is on its way, so we change course and head up Observation Point Trail, where we look out over the Upper Geyser Basin and watch Old Faithful erupt from above.

"Every corner brings another vibrant geothermal pool, bubbling mud pit, or steaming geyser."

58

YOSEMITE NATIONAL PARK

A Nature Lover's Paradise

Yosemite National Park has a reputation for being one of the most beautiful places on the planet. With its impressive granite walls, cascading waterfalls, and lush meadows, it's not hard to see why. The park is open year-round, but best explored in May through July when the waterfalls are flowing, the meadows are lush and green, and the trails are mostly snow-free. Yosemite can get very busy, so it's advisable to visit midweek for smaller crowds and less traffic in the Valley. Another way to avoid the crowds is to explore slightly less frequented areas, such as Tuolumne Meadows, Mariposa Grove, and various backcountry trails.

LOCATION California
PARK SIZE 747,946 acres
ICONIC FEATURE Tunnel View overlook
BEST SEASON Spring and summer

VISIT TIME Highlights in 2-3 days, or best explored in 5 days
STAY Half Dome Village cabins or canvas tents
MUST HIKE Mist Trail to Nevada Falls
PHOTO TIP Capture sunset over Half Dome at either Glacier Point or Tunnel View, made famous by photographer Ansel Adams.

It's late September as we wake in our tent to the Sierra Nevada's first dusting of snow. The stillness of the mountains feels almost palpable, and we marvel at the peacefulness and sheer beauty of the Cathedral Lakes valley. The fierce Californian sun melts most of the snow by end of day, and our backpacking trip continues. It has always been a dream of ours to summit Half Dome and we are among the lucky 300 people given a daily permit for the following day. Our muscles burn and feet slip as we traverse the worn granite of Half Dome's final ascent. All the pain is instantly forgotten when we stand at the summit to breathtaking views over the Yosemite Valley and beyond.

"It is by far the grandest of all the special temples of nature I was ever permitted to enter."

– John Muir

59

ZION NATIONAL PARK

A Treasure Of The Southwest

Zion is one of the most beautiful national parks in the country, and for that reason more than 4.5 million visitors explore its wonders each year. Famous for its picturesque hikes, slot canyons, and towering red canyon walls, Zion really has something to please any visitor. Popular activities in the park include hiking, backpacking, canyoneering, rock climbing, photography, bicycling, birding, camping, horseback riding, and kayaking. Summer can be incredibly busy and it's worth considering a visit during shoulder seasons, or even in winter.

LOCATION Utah
PARK SIZE 146,597 acres
ICONIC FEATURE Angels Landing and the Narrows
BEST SEASON Spring and fall
VISIT TIME Highlights in 2 days, or best explored in 4 days
STAY Camp at the South Campground, or stay in luxury at Zion Lodge.
MUST HIKE Observation Point and the Subway trails
PHOTO TIP Photograph the Watchman from Canyon Junction at sunset, and hike out to the Wall Street section of the Narrows for endless photo opportunities.

Silence. That's all there is as we sit watching a beautiful sunrise from Observation Point. Looking down into Zion Canyon, we can see the valley starting to come to life, and within hours the shuttle buses will begin, and our peace will be over. It was a grueling upward climb of some 2,000 ft / 610 m with our camping gear the afternoon before. As we set up camp along the East Rim Trail, we were relieved to be away from the crowds and able to enjoy sunset and sunrise at Observation Point mostly to ourselves. Even the busiest parks can be enjoyed in solitude… You just have to know where to go.

"Silence. That's all there is as we sit watching a beautiful sunrise from Observation Point... Even the busiest parks can be enjoyed in solitude... You just have to know where to go."

Arches

SOUTHWEST PARKS ITINERARY

The Grand Circle Road Trip

The Grand Circle is a popular national parks road trip, and for good reason. The southwest is bursting with stunning scenery, unique hikes, and classic Americana vibes. This trip is best experienced in two to three weeks, with the option of extending the adventure by visiting various optional side trips.

BEGIN – Las Vegas
01 ZION
02 BRYCE CANYON
03 CAPITOL REEF
04 CANYONLANDS
05 ARCHES
06 GRAND CANYON
END – Las Vegas

OPTIONAL SIDE TRIPS
Valley of Fire State Park, Monument Valley Navajo Tribal Park, Dead Horse Point State Park, Grand Staircase-Escalante National Monument, Antelope Canyon and Horseshoe Bend.

BEST OF THE WEST ITINERARY

A Multi-Month Epic Adventure

We understand that not everyone can dedicate half a year or more to explore all the national parks. This 'Best of the West' road trip would be an incredible two to three-month long adventure for those wishing to experience some of the best parks in the country in a more condensed time frame.

BEGIN - San Francisco
01 LASSEN VOLCANIC
02 REDWOODS
03 CRATER LAKE
04 OLYMPIC
05 MOUNT RAINIER
06 NORTH CASCADES
07 GLACIER
08 YELLOWSTONE
09 GRAND TETON
10 ROCKY MOUNTAIN
11 ARCHES
12 CANYONLANDS
13 CAPITOL REEF
14 BRYCE CANYON
15 ZION
16 GRAND CANYON
17 DEATH VALLEY
18 SEQUOIA
19 KINGS CANYON
20 YOSEMITE
END - San Francisco

Yellowstone

Mount Rainier

WASHINGTON PARKS ITINERARY

Diverse Beauty

We may be biased; we do live here, after all… but the Pacific Northwest has some of the best scenery in the country. If you only have a week or two, this trip is sure to make your jaw drop. From rugged coastline to lush rainforest, towering peaks, and the tallest volcano in the lower 48 states, this trip is sure to leave you awestruck.

BEGIN – Seattle
01 OLYMPIC
02 MOUNT RAINIER
03 NORTH CASCADES
END – Seattle

OPTIONAL SIDE TRIPS

Mount Baker Wilderness, Glacier Peak Wilderness, Leavenworth, Mount St. Helens, Goat Rocks Wilderness

LEAVE NO TRACE

How To Responsibly Enjoy The Parks

We are all so incredibly privileged to be able to enjoy natural spaces like those protected by the National Park Service. As visitors and humans who care about the future of our planet, it is our responsibility to enjoy the outdoors in a sustainable way and leave as little negative impact as possible. Before visiting the parks, be sure to educate yourself on the Leave No Trace Seven Principles:

PLAN AHEAD AND PREPARE
TRAVEL AND CAMP ON DURABLE SURFACES
DISPOSE OF WASTE PROPERLY
LEAVE WHAT YOU FIND
MINIMIZE CAMPFIRE IMPACTS
RESPECT WILDLIFE
BE CONSIDERATE OF OTHER VISITORS

Lake Clark

Glacier Bay

“Within National Parks is room – glorious room – room in which to find ourselves, in which to think and hope, to dream and plan, to rest and resolve.”

– Enos Mills

ACKNOWLEDGEMENTS

Firstly, we would like to extend a sincere thank you to everyone who has helped create and protect our national parks throughout the years, and for those who continue to do so every day. Thank you to the native people of these parks who shared their land with us and to the locals who graciously taught us about their cultures.

A massive thank you to everyone who followed our national parks journey on social media and who have further supported us by purchasing this book. We have felt so encouraged having you along for the ride and very much appreciate your kind comments and thoughtful messages.

Thank you to our amazing publisher—Lannoo—and the team who worked on Roaming America. You were the first to suggest we create this book, believed in us from the start, and did an incredible job bringing our vision to life.

To our friends at Evolve, thank you for sending us on this life-changing road trip. We are honoured that you chose us to support your brand and bring more awareness to protecting the national parks. In particular, thank you to Uwe Zens and Jason Hull for everything you did to make this trip happen.

Thank you to the wonderful team at Go Westy for trusting us with Ruby. She was the backbone of this trip, and we will forever be thankful for the places she took us and the many lessons we learned from her along the way. Thank you to Jad Josey and everyone in the repairs team for always being there for us whenever we had a van-related question.

Thank you to our friend Erin Sullivan for joining us in Alaska during a time of need; you were a tremendous support. Thank you to the many other friends of ours who we spent time with along the way, who joined us on a hike, or offered us a hot shower or a place to stay the night. Thank you to our amazing friend Emma Osmanski, who supported us throughout the year with a pseudo-home to send our mail and for being a friend we can always rely on.

To everyone we met during the trip and who took the time to share their stories, thank you. A special mention to Ira Wolf, Geoffrey Glassner, Gary Titus, the Alsworth family, Lukasz Stachowiak, and Jule Harle for adding such value to our journey.

Thank you to our wonderful families, who supported us every step of the way. Your video calls kept us grounded and were a much-needed reprieve during some tough moments on the road. We are forever grateful for the love and encouragement you have given us and the sacrifices you have made for our benefit over the years. Thank you for always being our loudest cheerleaders!

Lastly, we would both like to thank each other for sharing this incredible journey. It wasn't always easy living and working together 24/7 in a tiny van, but we made it work. We grew so much as individuals and as a couple during those seven months and throughout the process of creating this book, and for that we are immensely thankful.

Renee + Matthew

COLOPHON

www.lannoo.com

Sign up for our newsletter with news about new and forth coming publications on art, interior design, food & travel, photography and fashion as well as exclusive offers and events.

Authors: Renee and Matthew Hahnel
@ReneeRoaming
@MatthewHahnel

reneeroaming.com
matthewhahnel.com

Editing: Joy Philips
Photography: Renee and Matthew Hahnel
Graphic design: Diederik Serlet

If you have any questions or comments about the material in this book, please do not hesitate to contact our editorial team: art@lannoo.com

D/2019/45/283 – NUR 500/513
ISBN: 978 94 014 5348 6
9th print run